THE REAL WORK

THE
REAL
WORK

✦

*On the Mystery
of Mastery*

Adam Gopnik

Liveright Publishing Corporation

*A Division of W. W. Norton & Company
Celebrating a Century of Independent Publishing*

For information about permission to reproduce selections from
this book, write to Permissions, Liveright Publishing Corporation,
a division of W. W. Norton & Company, Inc.,
500 Fifth Avenue, New York, NY 10110

For information about special discounts for bulk purchases,
please contact W. W. Norton Special Sales at
specialsales@wwnorton.com or 800-233-4830

Manufacturing by Lakeside Book Company
Book design by Lovedog Studio
Production manager: Anna Oler

ISBN 978-1-324-09075-5

Liveright Publishing Corporation
500 Fifth Avenue, New York, N.Y. 10110
www.wwnorton.com

W. W. Norton & Company Ltd.
15 Carlisle Street, London W1D 3BS

1 2 3 4 5 6 7 8 9 0

For everyone who teaches, and anyone who'll learn

And in continuing memory of the greatest teacher
I've ever known, or will know,
Kirk Varnedoe

CONTENTS

✦

CONTENTS

THE REAL WORK

Introduction

MAGICIANS HAVE A BEAUTIFUL TERM. OVER late-night drinks in New York, or over three a.m. breakfasts in Las Vegas, they love to talk to each other about "the real work": who has it? Who got it? Who keeps it going?

Now, magicians have the most entrancing, the most *rapturous*, shop talk of any people I've ever known. There's a simple reason for that: the only people they're allowed to talk about their craft with are other magicians. Their technique has to be, as one of the best of them has said, not transparent, as in the other arts, but invisible. Invisible technique can be made audible only to the other masters of invisibility.

When they talk about the "real work," magicians mean the accumulated craft, savvy, and technical mastery that makes a great magic trick great. When they ask each other, "Who's got the real work on that?" about an illusion or effect, it doesn't mean who thought of it first or even who does it most adeptly but rather: who first mastered the whole of the handling, and timing and theatrics of the effect? Who knew to put the elephant sideways in the big box or to pause before the shuffle, all of the exquisitely small but significant steps that make something beautiful, not a dutiful dumb trick—you're fooled, sure, but you don't care—which are passed along from magician to magician and from generation to generation? The real work is the complete activity, the accumulated practice, and the total summing up of traditions. The real work is what makes a magic effect magical.

We all know the real work in whatever field it is we've mastered. It's shorthand, one might say, for the difference between accomplishment and mere achievement, the assigned work. When you introduce or even just drop the concept into conversation, it meets immediate nods of recognition. George Plimpton, in one of his books on football, tells the story of how, at a Pro Bowl practice, the players naturally, and without intervention by the coaches or argument from one another, sorted out into first team, second team, and so on. They knew.

Yet the real work doesn't seem to be a goal of the way we live, which favors, over the real work, what we might call the rote work. We live in an achievement-driven society in which kids of all kinds and classes (though in particular fortunate ones from fortunate families) are perpetually being pushed toward the next evanescent achievement instead of the next enduring accomplishment. A kind of mad Red Queen's contest happens as a consequence: we invent achievement tests that will be completely immune to coaching, and therefore we have ever more expensive coaches to break the code of the non-coachable achievement test. We drive our kids typically toward achievement, and yet anyone who is a parent of any sensitivity at all recognizes that what really stirs and moves children, just as it stirs and moves ourselves, isn't achievement, isn't the "A" you get on the test or the score you get on the SATs, however instrumental that may be to some larger ambition. No, what really moves and stirs us is *accomplishment*, that moment of mastery when suddenly we feel that something profoundly difficult, tenaciously thorny, has given way, and we are now the Master of It, instead of us being mastered *by* it. Even writers—especially writers—know that moment. One of my friends refers to it as the moment when his little inner namesake, call him "Dave," appears, coming out of nowhere to write the essay much better than David can. That feeling may not be the very best feeling in life—there are a few competitive others— but it is, I've come to believe, the most sustaining feeling. *I know how to do this, and this is the thing I know how to do.*

And so I wanted to study the nature of accomplishment, and more broadly what I like to call the mystery of mastery, both the long processes of how the real work installs itself inside of us and the single moments of mastery in which we do, somehow, face the music. How is it that we go about mastering difficult things? Better put: how is that we find ourselves, a year or so into learning to produce the Erdnase color change in a deck of cards, changing red for black, or how to play George Shearing songs on the piano, able to do things we didn't think we could do?

———

I STUMBLED RETROSPECTIVELY on the sequence this book presents. It begins with my effort, after thirty years as an art critic, making vast pronunciamientos on other people's drawings, to actually attempt to draw a single nude body myself, and then goes on to other enterprises, some lesser, some larger. Mastery as a critic obviously means something different from what it does to an artist. We can easily imagine an art critic with no hands, just as we know—uneasy truth— the first art historian, Lomazzo, was blind. And the same is true for every other skill: doing it well is different from judging it eloquently.

For the longest time, that difference did not seem to me to be vitally important. After all, the artist makes, the critic criticizes, and while one resents the other, they circle each other warily, engaged in different kinds of work. Yet I came to see, in drawing as much as in boxing and dancing, that we miss the whole if we don't attempt to grasp, in however limited and even feeble a form, what the real work feels like for other people as they do it. A sportswriter doesn't have to be able to hit a baseball thrown by a Major League pitcher, but without some sense of what that act *feels* like—the hand and eye coordination of it, the satisfaction of the consequent thwack, however rare—she doesn't grasp what batting *is*. Pick out a Gershwin melody on the piano, and one has a much stronger sense of the astounding things that Erroll Garner is capable of than listening alone can offer. Fingers know, or rather don't know, things that ears cannot. The great art historian E. H. Gombrich, with a vast, panascopic view of art, once said that as he aged, or let's say ripened, the skill, alien to him, that it took for an artist to draw a single blade of grass seemed to him ever-more astounding. Doing something well for a lifetime actually teaches us less about what the real work is than doing something badly can teach us when we start doing it anew. Everybody's good at *something*. Being bad at something reminds us of how we ever got good at anything.

Still one more lesson was implicit in that one. Everyone is good at something, yes, but what I perceived in apprenticing myself to masters in various fields is that we are surrounded by masters. I don't mean the world-class saxophone player one might fail to recognize on the subway. I mean something more mundane. I mean the mastery all around us, all the time.

———

EVERYONE, I THINK, has a moment when we learn to do things that not only seem difficult but impossible until you began to do them. Reading is, perhaps, the key one in our society, where the act of deciphering meaningless marks on white backgrounds into stories, formulas, lessons, erotic stimulation, begins early and governs all else. If we're lucky, we can just recall the feeling of looking at a meaningless series of marks and then beginning the work of decoding them. I remember learning to read out loud, and, encountering the word "knife," the precise moment when the mystery of that disquieting and unwelcome *k*, preceding the phonetically sensible "nife," got solved. You saw it but didn't say it. Having to accept the *k* to get the sense, and the image, seemed to me the type of the kind of cognitive compromise we make in mastering anything.

Though I was a good reader at a young age, my conscious sense of mastery came from seeing people do things that my own always poorly coordinated hands and eyes could not. The concept of accomplishment seems intuitively tied to our ability to do difficult things; the concept of *mastery* seems tied to things that look downright impossible until we see them done. We all have a sliding scale of mastery: what looks absurdly easy to some of us (speaking in public extemporaneously) looks impossible to others, and what looks easy (climbing the sheer rock face of a mountainside) looks, God knows, utterly impossible to the people who know how to talk in front of a crowd. Just writing the words makes me tremble.

I was already in awe in kindergarten of girls who could keep neat three-ring binders, or tie shoes successfully, a thing I still can't do reliably. (I married one who can.) Above all, I was conscious of my mother as a source of evident mastery, of making hard things look easy, but making impossible things look fluid. My first memory of mastery is of watching my mother make strudel. My older sister Alison and I would sit beneath the round table in the public housing project where we were growing aware, and our parents were starting out in life, and snatch at the bits and pieces of dough that hung over the edge as my mother smoothed the dough out impossibly fine, running over it again and again until, when we emerged to look, it was thinner than paper-parchment, and far from being torn as she rolled it over, remained sufficiently plastic to stay in place.

Recalling the act now, I understand that I did not have the *concepts* of any of this—the idea that materials had plasticity and could be made thin without being made brittle—but was duly impressed, not just that it was happening but that it was happening through entirely physical means, that it was happening as an act of earned skill, not strange maternal magic—except of course, that earned skill is strange maternal magic. (I recall my own son, Luke, having seen his mother suddenly appear at the shuttered window on a Parisian street to call out a request as we set out for the market, looking warily at every other window on the succeeding streets, in expectation, or hope, that she would appear in them again.)

The awe at the mastery, of being able to make strudel dough that thin and then turn it into strudel, impressed me even more than the strudel, of which I have a dimmer recollection. Many years later, seeing a baker on the Greek islands roll out his dough across cool marble, even finer than my mother had, I was only impressed with the certainty that he, too, had had a mother. (I asked him; he had.) It may be that my own latter-day sense that mastery resides in kitchens began with my mother, though it is certainly true that if there is one arena in which the acts of mastery are most easily studied by ordinary people, it's cooking, where, over years, even the most ham-handed of us amateur chefs learn to do things that seemed impossible when we started trying and that now are part of a nightly, wine-fueled flow of inevitabilities. My sister, under that table with me, carried through her the superseding conviction in her work as a developmental psychologist that our understanding had been much lamed by the perpetual dismissal of the natural experiments of life, in watching children or making dinner, for instance, to be mere women's work. Perhaps much of what we call the real work is women's work made real.

Not to reduce my mother, or any mother, to a mom. She was always, as she would be the first to tell you, and then remind you again, a logician and a linguist, given to science more than cooking craft. Yet if I itemize my own first experience of the real work, it comes from her hands, despite many difficulties we might have had later, and my own reservations about the character traits we shared. She rolled strudel, and then later traced for me the rudiments of Gödel's Proof on a beach, and then taught me step by step how to make a beef Stroganoff, my favorite dish at twelve—steps (onions, peppers, beef, sauce, sour cream) that I not only know by heart and execute today but that were, perhaps, my first conscious induction into the deeper truth, which the stories in this book recapitulate: that mastery happens small step by small step and that the mystery, more often than not, is that of a kind of life-enhancing equivalent of the illusion called "persistence of motion" when we watch a movie or cartoon. "Flow" is the shorthand term that's been popularized for the feeling of the real work as it seeps through our neurons and veins, and, though we may know the flow of some things we do so well by middle age that we scarcely feel them flowing, having to set out on a new current makes us feel the resistance that is essential to the motion. "Flow," we learn again, always begins as fragments. The separate steps become a sequence, and the sequence then looks like magic, or just like life, or just like Stroganoff.

————

FROM DRAWING NUDE BODIES BADLY, I went on to driving a car nervously and then to doing, or at least admiring, magic tricks awkwardly while dancing even more awkwardly than that, our feet (or, at least my feet) being more recalcitrant than our (or my) hands. And all the while the joy of music making hovered above, as a dream, and occasionally a gig. Each episode arose out of emotional moment more than the purposeful plan: I needed at last to learn to drive to relieve my wife, and I wanted to re-cement a relationship with my daughter by dancing.

But the force of what was happening as, mostly unplanned, I found that learning one skill after another was cumulative and mutually reinforcing. In midlife we become less able but more aware, and I was aware, for the first time, of the fiendish difficulty of doing impossible-looking things well, and of the fiendish reward of even doing them badly. Each episode taught a lesson, and at the end the storyteller's goal, Scheherazade's life potion—a point—seemed to hover in the distance.

I've tried not to sum up too neatly the point or moral of each adventure as it happened. One of the biggest points of all is that every accomplishment is rooted in a practice. You master it by the totality of what you're doing. One can reduce a sauce to its essence, but you have to be careful not to cook off the alcohol entirely.

Still, three themes seem to spiral out, educating me as they emerged. First, again, that the flow is always a function of fragments, fluid sequences are made of small steps. Separate, discrete actions learned by effort and then put together give not just the illusion of unity but the fact of mastery. The great sociologist and piano player Howie Becker calls these "crips," in reference to learning jazz piano in strip clubs in Chicago in the nineteen forties. Crips were pre-formed "shapes"—figures on the piano that could be strung together into inspired improvisations, not less inspired for not being entirely improvised. The art was to take the received pieces and string them into a new whole. It does not diminish Lester Young to say that he often played the same swooping figure in each minor blues; it was finding the right place to put the same swooping figure in every number that made him Lester Young.

Second, that everything we do involves everything we do. Every brush mark we make, every note we play, every sentence we craft—every left turn we take into traffic!—betrays and engages the totality of ourselves and even of our time. We search in the arts not simply for the signs of skill, which are, if not easily taught, still teachable. We search for the signs of a unique human presence: it's why we love vibrato in a voice, legato in piano performance, why we catalog the tics and mannerisms of a baseball player at bat—Joe Morgan's way of rotating his arm like a wing—as much as we watch his numbers. It's why, even after the miracle of illusion and perspective has been mastered, we can still learn to know, at a glance, a seventeenth-century drawing from an eighteenth-century one. We never really love an artist's virtuosity, or if we do, it feels empty. We love their vibrato, their unique way of entangling their learned virtuosity within their unique vulnerability.

And finally, that when we look to understand mastery what

we find are masters—moms and dads, brothers and sisters, teachers and tutors, men and women who are, often for the most eccentric of reasons or with the most improbably eccentric practices and teaching methods, able to impart something of what they know. The people I was blessed to bump into along the way are not mere repositories of knowledge but living exemplars of a practice.

The thing about the humanities is that they're human. And human means specific, this guy or girl right here. The deeper we dive into the problem of mastery, the more certain we are to meet a master—a man or woman uniquely good at what they do, and sometimes able to break it down and share it. My mother rolling out strudel dough was engaged in something that was a knack, a trick, a tradition, an accomplishment, and a gift, an act of sharing. It was a humane act in the fact of being human.

When we search for the real work, what we find are not life rules but real lives. Learning to drive is learning to understand your father, just as learning the Erdnase color change with cards implies, and implicates you in, a complicated history of long vanished railroad cars where card men would cheat one another at the risk of their lives. We can hear the swaying and clacking of the old trains when we do it now.

———

I HAVE WOUND this book around Seven Mysteries of Mastery that exemplify or illuminate the crafts, coming as fables that point (or once or twice come at right angles) to our subject. Some of these are sidebars, some prefaces, a few expanded footnotes. I arrived at the number seven by accident—they were what I had—only to discover, or perhaps be reminded, that seven is *always* the number of mysteries, including the seven mysteries of Faith, and the seven sacraments—a serendipity that might be explained as reflecting the mystical clockwork of creation, or might, instead be explained by the dumb capacities of the filing cabinet of our mind, reflecting George Miller's famous discovery that the human mind has a capacity for seven items, give or take two, and strains to reach for more.

Or, it could be both at once? The dumb limits of the filing cabinet in our cognition are also the cipher to unlock the stars. The capacity of that seven-digit space in our mind, the most mundane imaginable weakness of a human brain that is, after all, not divinely engineered but made up catch as catch can by an evolutionary history—that does what it can from what's lying around—supplies us a springboard and a kind of resonance. We take advantage of the constraints and limitations of what we have in order to leap to what we want. We are not limited by our limitations. Again and again in these stories, we'll see those constraints and limitations, far from crippling us, are the source and the goad and the ground of the mastery we seek.

I realized, as I worked on these pages, that what I was writing was a self-help book that won't help. Won't help, I mean, in the shallow sense of helping you immediately to do the things the book is about doing better. It offers no shortcuts or bullet points and provides no recipes—except one or two for sourdough bread. Yet I hope that it might help you better see yourself *as* a self, a constructed self, made out of appetites turned into accomplishments. We are all LEGO creatures, built of small, bright blocks, with knobs and holes to connect them, and if we could see ourselves as we really are, we would recognize that our hats and smiles are simple add-ons to that repeated architecture of red and green bricks, assembled, if not by the hand of God, then by our own hands since childhood.

Very often, moments of meaning—what we call epiphanies—are simply the sudden illumination of all those points in the network of loves and lives, lighting up at once. For a moment of vision, as makers or observers, the totality of things is apparent to us. And we say, *Listen to that. Look at that. That works!* It's a mystical feeling—*the* mystical feeling, actually—but it's the end of a multitude of labors, some of which we may not even know we've started until they rise to startle us, may not know we've undertaken until after they've overtaken us. We know it when it happens. It's the real work.

The First Mystery
of Mastery

*The Turk, or, The Mystery
of Performance*

D OING BEGINS BY DOUBTING. THAT'S ONE OF the great lessons we inherit from the scientific tradition. So before we start to do, let us start to doubt. And we can doubt by considering the case of one of the great doubt-provokers of the Enlightenment: the Turk. It was, as you may know, the first great automaton—a chess-playing machine that inflamed Europe in the late eighteenth century. That it was not actually an automaton and couldn't play chess didn't alter the effect it had on people at the time. Like many others, I have been fascinated by the Turk since I first read about it, in histories of magic and illusion. Then Tom Standage's fine 2002 horizontal social history of the machine and its times, called, simply, *The Turk*, clarified an often deliberately mystified history.

The Turk first appeared in Vienna in 1770 as a chess-playing machine—a mechanical figure of a bearded man dressed in Turkish clothing, seated above a cabinet with a chessboard on top. Its inventor and first operator, a Hungarian quasi-nobleman, scientist, and engineer named Wolfgang von Kempelen—one of those amazing Enlightenment figures who danced at eight weddings at once and still kept the beat—would assemble a paying audience, open the doors of the lower cabinet, and show the impressively whirring clockwork mechanisms that filled the inner compartments beneath the seated figure. Then he would close the cabinet and invite a challenger to play chess. The automaton—the robot, as we would say now—would gaze at the opponent's move, ponder, then raise its mechanical arm and make a stiff but certain move of its own. Mastery had been implanted in it; a computer, a living brain, had been taught somehow to play chess!

Before it was destroyed by fire in Philadelphia in the 1850s, the Turk toured Europe and America and played games with everyone from Benjamin Franklin to, by legend at least, Napoleon Bonaparte. It certainly once played a game with Philidor, the greatest chess master of the age. The Turk lost, but Philidor admitted that he had been hard-pressed to defeat it, a public relations triumph for Kempelen. Artificial intelligence, the eighteenth century believed, had arrived, wearing a fez and ticking away like Captain Hook's crocodile.

Of course, the thing was a fraud, or rather, a trick—a clever magician's illusion. A sliding sled on well-lubricated casters had been fitted inside the lower cabinet and the only real ingenuity was how this simple machine allowed a hidden chess player to glide easily, and silently, into a semi-seated position inside. There was a lot more room to hide in the cabinet than all that clockwork machinery suggested.

Now, the Turk fascinates me for several reasons, since it illuminates many odd and haunting holes in human reasoning and in our response to mastery. It reminds us, in Ottoman garb, that mastery is, among other things, a *performance*, and one that depends on our guesses, confident or not, about the identity of the master we're watching.

The first truth it embodied is that, once impressed, we quickly leave the ladder of incremental reasoning behind. Common sense should have told the people who watched and challenged it that for the Turk to have *really* been a chess-playing machine, it would have had to have been the latest in a long sequence of such machines. For there to be a mechanical Turk who played chess, there would have had to have been, ten years before, a mechanical Greek who played checkers. It's true that the late eighteenth century was a great age of automatons, machines that could make programmed looms weave and mechanical birds sing— although always the same song, or tapestry, over and over. But the reality that chess-playing was an entirely different kind of creative activity seemed as obscure to them as it seems obvious to us now.

People were fooled because they were looking, as we always seem to do, for the elegant and instant solution to a problem, even when the cynical and ugly and incremental one is right. The great-grandfather of computer science, Charles Babbage, saw the Turk, and though he realized that it was probably a magic trick, he also asked himself what exactly would be required to produce an elegant solution. What kind of machine would you actually have to build if you could build a machine to play chess? What would its capacities need to be? Babbage's "difference engine"— the first computer—arose in part from his desire to believe that there was a beautiful solution to the problem of what we now call artificial intelligence, even if the one before him was not it.

We always want not just the right solution to a mystery; we want a *beautiful* solution. And when we meet a mysterious thing, we are always inclined to believe that it must therefore conceal an inner beauty. When we see an impregnable tower, we immediately are sure that there must be a princess inside. Doubtless there are many things that seem obscure to us—the origins of the universe, the nature of consciousness, the possibility of time travel—that will seem obvious in the future. But the solutions to their obscurity, too, will undoubtedly be clunky and ugly and more ingenious than sublime. The solution to the problem of consciousness will involve, so to speak, sliding sleds and hidden chess players.

———

BUT THERE IS another aspect of the thing that haunts me too. Though some sought a beautiful solution when a cynical one was called for, plenty of people—Edgar Allan Poe, for instance, who wrote a long analytic piece on the machine when it toured America, one of his first significant published works—realized that the Turk had to be what it actually was, a cabinet with a chess player inside. What seems to have stumped Poe and the other, shrewder Turk detectives was not the ugliness of the solution but the singularity of the implied chess player. Where would you find a tiny chess genius, they wondered. Or could the operator be using fiendishly well-trained children? Even if you accepted the idea of an adult player, who could it be, this hidden, inscrutable but unquestionable *master*?

It turns out that the chess players who operated the Turk from inside were just . . . chess players, an ever-changing sequence of strong but not star players, who needed the gig badly enough to be willing to spend a week or a month working sessions inside its smoky innards. Kempelen, and then after him a traveling showman named Maelzel, who bought and restored the automaton and took it to America, picked up chess players wherever they happened to be, as Chuck Berry used to hire his backup bands on the road. In Paris, when the Turk played Philidor, Kempelen recruited a variety of strong but second-rank chess players from places like the Café de la Régence, the leading chess café in a city where coffeehouse life had bloomed to become a separate civil society of its own. They included a surprisingly tall player named Boncourt; a chess writer named Alexandre; and a now completely unknown chess player named Weyle.

For this was the most astonishing of Kempelen's insights, a sublime shortcut every bit as brilliant in its way as actually building a chess-playing machine. It was that, in the modern world, *mastery was widely available*. None of the names of the chess masters who played as the Turk were particularly remarkable then or famous now. They were students, second-rank players, not an enslaved little person or an inspired child among them. Merely strong chess players who needed the work—badly enough to put up with the discomforts and absurdities of slipping inside the Turk. The operators never lacked for someone to play the role. There was always someone available who was good enough to win, needed the gig, and didn't mind the working conditions. They would take the job and get inside the machine, get paid for it, and the Turk would move on to its next stop in Boston or Bruges, and Kempelen or Maelzel would go to another chess club and ask, Does anyone who isn't claustrophobic need a job? At one point, on board a boat taking the invention to America, Maelzel actually recruited a young French girl who had never played chess before and taught her a series of endgames. Chess players assure me that these are easier to play than it might seem, but they were still hard enough to add a note of risk.

Kempelen was a genius, certainly. But his genius didn't lay in programming a machine that was capable of playing chess. His genius was that he understood the ubiquity of mastery. In a world seeking excellence, with millions of people crowded into competitive cities, excellence becomes surprisingly well distributed. The second-best chess player at a chess club is a far better chess player than you can imagine.

And therein lies what I think of now as the asymmetry of mastery: we overrate masters and underrate mastery. With the Turk, the simplest solution was the hardest, partly because those in the audience underestimated the space inside the cabinet but also because they overestimated just how good the chess player had to be. We always overestimate the space between the very good and the uniquely good. That inept soccer player we whistle at in despair is a better soccer player than we will ever meet. The few people who do grasp the asymmetry of mastery, tend, like Kempelen and Maelzel, to profit greatly from it. The greatest managers in any sport are those who know you can always find new and "lesser" players to play a vital role.

The sociologist Howie Becker tried to systematize this insight. The distinctive thing about "creativity," in his view, is not that it's rare but that it's so *common*, if often misidentified. Some of the most seemingly creative professions—for instance, playing classical music with an orchestra—are in fact the most routinized and rule-bound; others that we typically don't even count as creative—such as a woman at home cooking for her family (he was writing in the 1950s)—face new predicaments and find genuinely creative solutions. As with my mother, the mastery itself is not difficult; recognizing it, organizing it, rewarding it, *that's* the difficult part, and often subject to haphazard prejudice, not to mention, of course, deeply implanted bigotries and social oppressions, of the kind that reduced many brilliant, inspired home cooks to the status of "housewife."

My son, Luke, was obsessed with card magic as an adolescent but, having learned that art, he realized the fundamental human truth: that girls are not impressed by card tricks. They like guitar players. He spent several years "mastering" guitar, as he had once "mastered" chess and then card magic. Then we went to a party where a jazz combo had been dressed by the party-givers in ridiculous 1920s-style clothing. Luke pointed to a guitarist in his ludicrous spats and Gatsby hat, forced for money to clock ticky-tacky chords, and said, "Dad, that man is a much better guitar player than anyone I have ever played with." It was the chess-café phenomenon. Mastery is available, and in need of work.

And what of the handful of true, undisputed masters? What makes them unique, I've come to think, is not so much virtuosity but instead some strange idiosyncratic vibration of his or her own. What we call genius is most often inspired idiosyncrasy, and sometimes even inspired idiocy. Bob Dylan started off as a bad musician, and then spent 10,000 hours practicing. But he did not become a better musician. He became Bob Dylan. And it should be said that some of those who possess ultimate mastery, as Bobby Fischer and Michael Jackson conspire to remind us, have hollow lives of surpassing unhappiness, as if the needed space for a soul were replaced by whirring clockwork. Perhaps our children sense this truth as they struggle to master things.

Those who stand out in a first rank rarely have a skill that can be defined technically. Even in the narrow and circumscribed region of chess, the geniuses who stand out have a different kind of gift—often referred to, inadequately, as "creative flair" or "situational intelligence." Hard work certainly matters. But a lot of people work hard. Wayne Gibson and the Tornadoes played the same clubs in Hamburg as the Beatles. Did they work less hard? Perhaps. They went on to sign a contract, record some flops, and then a hit or two with Beatles and Stones songs. Obviously, Wayne was less talented than Sir Paul. But being talented is also, obviously, a composite gift. It arrives each time in a unique formula of many parts, some obvious, some more mysterious.

Having so many masters around can be a comfort to even to minor ones. If excellence is insufficiently rewarded, it's less because the world is cruel than because it is so busy handing out rewards. There are just a lot of terrific pianists, amazing chess players, first-rate gymnasts, tennis players with astonishing backhands, short-story writers with a feeling for dialogue and the poignant arc. We tend to focus unduly on a handful of names because it simplifies life to do so. They can't all be champions. One of the joys I found in reading and editing the great jazz critic Whitney Balliett was to be exposed to those musicians who played in what he called "the shadows and shoals of show business," forgotten trombone players and "minor" pianists who nonetheless made high poetry literally out of thin, or more often, smoky air. Bill Coleman and Ed Bickert and Joe Bushkin—the integrity of their accomplishment is not diminished by the density of their kind, or the frequent invisibility of their legacy. They are there—once on LPs, now on Spotify—as masterly as ever, not unimportant, only momentarily unheard.

This is one reason why minor masters seek out the company of fellow aspirants to mastery, why those chess cafés in Paris were the place to search for Turk-inserts. The chess café, the nightclub after the show, the painters' salon—these are places where minor masters go to be known and seen for their mastery even if they can't be champions. It is good to sing in the great chorus of modern mastery and wait for our turn inside the machine.

There's a sadder side to this, as well, one that we struggle to explain to our kids, as I did with Luke about the guitar player. It is very hard to do a difficult thing, it is very important to learn to

THE FIRST MYSTERY OF MASTERY

do a difficult thing, and once you have learned to do it, you will always discover that there is someone else who does it better.

———

BUT OF ALL the reflections the Turk may inspire, still another is the most important. It was the orchestration of effects *around* the Turk that elevated the merely okay player to exceptional player. It was not the clockwork specificity of the machine but the totality of the effects—not the automaton itself but the atmosphere around it—that made the idea work, that gave the impression of mastery. The Turk was a physical frame in which a chess player could, however uncomfortably, play. But it was also a kind of psychological "frame," an envelope of expectations that magnified the power of the chess player inside.

For the other thing that Kempelen understood is that once you put a very good chess player into a very impressive-looking and mysterious-looking piece of machinery, he or she becomes a *great* chess player. Excellence always takes place within a context of performance. The power of the machine lay in how it urged people to project onto it powers that it never possessed, but that, by the act of sympathetic imagination, became possible, and, in a wonderful natural joke, eventually realized. Crediting the machine with more than it could do, the audience made the machine more credible. Who was inside the machine? You were.

Though a trick, the Turk wasn't a swindle. In its incapacity to do what it seemed to do, it prodded other people to do more. It was the essential nudge to Babbage in his thinking about the "difference engine." How could you achieve a chess-playing machine, make a real Turk? And it affected the history of literature. Poe's deductive account of the Turk, with its focus on the minutiae of performance and deception, became the model for his later detective stories, the first ever of their kind. The entire tradition of the detective story and all that it encompasses owes something to Poe's investigation of how the Turk might work. The idea of the "clue," which seems to us by now transparent and self-evident, had to be discovered. The idea that you could deduce responsibility by examining the residual traces of behavior—fingerprints or DNA, or in the case of the Turk the uses of the candelabra and the implications of magnetism—was a new one. By being opaque, the Turk helped launch that line of inquiry.

The story of art includes exactly the search for "cognitive prostheses" not unlike the Turk—for the formula, the advance, that makes art not merely accomplished but original. By "cognitive prostheses" we mean artificial extensions of our mind and senses that make them more powerful than they were unaided— some as simple as eyeglasses, some as complex as computer-assisted memory devices for the elderly with failing minds. Ben Franklin, after "inventing" or at least popularizing, bifocals in France, wrote in 1785 that the best thing about them was that he could both see what he was eating and watch the mouths of his companions: "When one's ears are not well accustomed to the sounds of a language, a sight of the movements in the features of him that speaks help to explain; so that I understand French better by the help of my spectacles." What seemed like an obvious perceptual prosthesis doubled as a subtler cognitive one.

But in a sense, all of the arts use such devices: even if we don't have a computer-assisted memory, mnemonic devices— like the famous "memory palaces" that many of us use to recall a sequence of thoughts for a lecture—or artistic practices, like the use of linear perspective to lay out a landscape according to a fixed rule, are cognitive prostheses as well. For that matter, so is the microphone we use to amplify a singing voice. "Speaking" singers, of the high order of Frank Sinatra, depend on a mic for their meanings. As much as eyeglasses let us see things we can't, or, as Franklin saw, "hear" better than we could, or a microphone lets us hear whispers we normally wouldn't, the grandeur of the imposture of the Turk made it seem something it wasn't.

———

THIS FIRST MYSTERY of mastery would seem to lead naturally to talking about magic tricks and their exemplary place in the real work. But I shall engage in a small bit of misdirection here and instead address first another kind of illusion, one that seems "higher" in our usual hierarchy of the arts. I mean perhaps the most original cognitive prosthesis that the Western world has invented: life and perspective drawing, the practice of making black marks on white paper that don't just seem to symbolize but actually resemble bodies and figures as we see them in the world. This is the realest of all work, with seemingly limitless horizons of meaning, from the most profound, where Michelangelo makes a human body a vessel for divine striving to the most basic, in the way that an erotic illustrator can turn hooks and scrawls into an activating object of desire. Yet it relies not on acuity of observation alone but on a set of tricks and techniques and trade secrets, on a series of cognitive prostheses so worn by time that they have the virtuous appearance of pure skill. It was my first dive into the extended practice of learning to do hard things I couldn't do before, and it brought me close to the first master I would consciously study *as a master*, even if I didn't quite realize it until later on. How does the work of art get real? It was a question only an artist could answer.

Drawing

IN THE MIDDLE OF THE JOURNEY OF MY LIFE, I decided to learn to draw. No, I wasn't lost in a dark, enclosing forest, but I *was* lost in the Manhattan equivalent: a midweek dinner party that had turned the corner to eleven thirty and now seemed likely never to end at all. The host was a terrific cook, but one of those seven-course terrific cooks, disappearing into the kitchen for a quarter of an hour at a time to execute the latest Ferran Adrià recipe while we all secretly gripped the underside of the dinner table, realizing that the babysitter meter was running and we would have to be up again in six hours to dress the kids and get them to school.

Having exhausted the exhausted neighbors to my left and right during the previous course breaks, I turned at last to my neighbor across the table. I knew that we had kids in the same school, and that he was married to the woman beside me. He was curly-haired and handsome in the pugilistic way that looks as though it ought to include a broken tooth. I asked him what he did.

"I'm an artist," he said. "A teacher. I teach people how to draw." He spoke with what I would come to recognize as a diffidence touched by, well, a certain touchiness, whose source I could not at that moment recognize or locate.

"Would you teach me how to draw?" I asked, for reasons that at the moment seemed as clear-flying as a lark in spring air, but that, over the next two years, receded and rose mysteriously, like fish swimming in a muddy aquarium.

"Sure," he said, only a little surprised. "Come by the studio." His name was Jacob Collins, and he explained that he supervised an "atelier" in midtown called the Grand Central Academy of Art. He knew that I wrote often about art, though the look on his face when he said it did not give the impression that he thought that what I wrote about was what anyone ought to call art.

Trying to negotiate the space between us, I said that I was going off to California to speak on Manet—did I intend that to be credentialing? I suppose I did—but that I would certainly come the week after. I had been writing about art, for a while officially as an "art critic" then after, when other subjects seemed more natural, as what might technically be called in Yiddish a *kunst-kibitzer*, a random weigher-in on the lives of painters, for decades. Nagging in the back of my mind had always been an urge to actually do this thing.

He seemed to stiffen, even wince, at the mention of the French painter's name. I might have said the man who painted the poker-playing dogs.

"You don't like Manet?" I said, wondering. Didn't everybody like Manet?

"Actually, I—" he began brutally, and then I thought I saw his wife, next to me, shoot him a perfect spousal "Don't start!" look, and he shrugged.

This was interesting. The realists I knew in the art world defended their occupation the way the religious believers I know defend theirs, as one more spiritual option within the liberal system: *See, I'm just exploring the possibilities of pluralism.* This was clearly something else. This guy really didn't like Manet!

When I got back from California, I armed myself with a sketchbook and a set of pencils and went to visit the Grand Central Academy of Art. The academy was in the same midtown building as the Mechanics Institute Library, a favorite retreat of mine already. I climbed the creaky wooden stairs, took a step into the atelier, and blinked. I was in a series of rooms that could have been found in Paris at the Académie in 1855 or, for that matter, in Rome in 1780. Easels everywhere, and among them plaster casts of classical statues, improbably white and grave and well muscled and oversized. The statues weren't displayed, as they are at the Met, at dignified intervals, but bunched together higgledy-piggledy, so that the effect was that of a cocktail party of tall white plaster people who worked out a lot. The Discus Thrower frowned and threw his discus; a Venus wrapped herself up modestly; an Apollo looked toward the Korean delis and salad bars just below; an incomplete David, with his slingshot, gazed into the distance. The scene was almost too much like one's mental image of it, as though a student interested in New York politics had opened the door to a downtown clubhouse and found corpulent, cigar-smoking politicians in porkpie hats and short-hemmed pants and vests with "Tammany" written in bleeding type across them.

A cluster of students in mildly worn jeans worked on their drawings. Each hand moved, back and forth, up and down from the wrist, and the world seemed to flow onto the sketcher's paper like silver water taking the form of things seen, subtle gradations of gray and black that didn't just notate the things in an expressive shorthand but actually mirrored them, in a different medium and on a different scale.

Jacob had someone set me up with an easel, and then gave me a small plaster cast of an eye—something taken from a statue perhaps three times life-size. "Just try and copy that," he said.

I held my pencil tight and began. I had a graduate degree in art history, and I *liked* to draw, though I did it very badly. I could make crude line-drawing faces, which, depending on the direction of the "eyebrows," might register vanity, conceit, worry, or anger. A squiggled line, for instance, drawn as a girl's eyes, looks like self-delight. If the hieroglyphs of emotion were that simple, how much harder, my modern-art-trained mind demanded, could the work of representation, mere mirroring, really be?

I stabbed at the paper, trying to copy the contour of the plaster eye, and then looked at what I had done. I had just made a hard line that limped awkwardly along the top of the page, enclosing a kind of egg shape, meant to be the pupil. I looked at the easels around me, at the play of shadow and shade, the real look of the thing, which seemed so natural. I flipped a page in my notebook and, gripping my pencil tighter and staring back at the eye, tried again. It was even worse, like a football inside a pair of parentheses.

After two more flipped pages, Jacob came over. In a gentle tone very different from his dinner-party manner, he said, "Yes, well . . . I would argue that the space you're asserting here in this corner could be seen as something much spacier. I think you could allow these intervals to . . ." He struggled for words. "To breathe more, without betraying the thing you're drawing." It was the most elaborately polite way possible of saying that the circle on the page meant to indicate the pupil was way too big in relation to the ridiculous double line meant to represent the orbit.

I started over on a new page and tried to stare the damn thing down. The plaster eye looked back at me opaquely, unforgivingly. I took a deep breath and tried to let my hand follow the line in front of me. But how did you distinguish the raised bits of the eye from the hollow bits, the ups from the downs? The light fell across the thing, creating darks and lights, but how to register these with a pencil point? I tried crosshatched shapes in the darker corners, but this made the eye look like a badly wrought Mayan numeral over which someone had scribbled tic-tac-toe boards. My chest tightened, and my breath came short. It was impossible.

As I crossed Sixth Avenue two hours later, I was filled with feelings of helplessness and stupidity and impotence that I had not experienced since elementary school. Why was I so unable to do something so painfully simple? Whatever sense of professional competence we feel in adult life is less the sum of accomplishment than the absence of impossibility: it's really our relief at no longer having to do things we were never any good at doing in the first place—relief at never again having to dissect a frog or memorize the periodic table. Much of what feels like mastery in adult life is actually the avoidance of a challenge. The "flow" in which, if we're lucky, our daily work is situated, is a narrow current within a broad river that we ceased navigating adventurously long ago, having capsized too many times to try again. The moment we steer back out, we're in white water, knuckles up. The feeling of impotent helplessness that all of us know from some piece of our early education—and that for the unlucky remains the dominant memory of schooling—is escaped not by becoming any less helpless but by doing only those things that don't need help.

Having to make a drawing that looks like the thing you're drawing was something I had given up not because I was too busy but because I was no good. I hadn't learned to draw because I had never been any good at drawing. Now I knew that I never would be. I tried to forget about the morning, and when I saw Jacob in the halls of our kids' school I exchanged brief, hooded, embarrassed looks with him, as one might with a failed blind date.

The little urge that had made me want to learn to draw was still intact, though, and, for the next six months, tugged on my insides like a bad conscience. Partly it was simple curiosity. *How do they do that trick?* Another reason was compensatory. For all the years I'd spent talking about pictures, the truth was that I had no real idea of how to draw or of what it felt like to do it. I would mistrust a poetry critic who couldn't produce a rhyming couplet. Could one write about art with *no* idea how to draw? It was true that the art I had written about was mostly of a kind that had stored life drawing away in the attic, as a youthful relic from summer camp. The older I got, though, the more I was pulled toward pure craft, unalloyed accuracy, the struggle to translate the surface of the world into a sentence or a sketch. And if I was going to study this thing I wanted to go there with a real hardass, not as the student of someone happily permissive. As the student of someone who thought there was one right way to do it and, even if that way was not mine, could at least show me what a way like that looks like.

Still, I would have let the plan to learn drawing molder in the pile of my unfulfilled ambitions—the pile that sits on the desk of life right next to the pile of escaped obligations—had I not bumped into Jacob one day at our kids' school, trapped in a corridor as he waited for a conference.

"Hey," he said. "If you're still interested, why don't you come around to my studio sometime and watch while I draw? We can just talk." And so that Friday I went over to his studio to watch him draw.

It was an old renovated stable and, in décor, was like a smaller version of the atelier—classical busts on shelves and even a hanging skeleton—but more intimate, and with Jacob's own sober paintings (a genial-looking older man, beautiful half-torsos of grave young women, a Berkshire winter landscape or two) hanging above our heads. There was a black Lab, who nuzzled visitors, and slept, and barked loudly when someone came to the door. Instead of the fluorescents of the atelier, there were jerry-rigged spots, small lamps clamped as needed to wooden pillars to throw a narrow tunnel of warm light on the object to be drawn, or, set wide, to make the light come raking across the model.

I liked it there, a lot. So, for the next year or so, I went often to the studio on Friday afternoons, and kept Jacob company as he drew in semi-darkness. Sometimes there was a skull or bust to draw, sometimes a naked person stretched out on a platform up front. I had an easel, to be sure, and would make a mark or two as I watched him work.

Jacob drew and drew and drew. His paintings had a somber, melancholic cast, in the manner of Thomas Eakins. But his drawings were prestidigitations, magical evocations of the thing seen, pencil drawings as accurate as photographs but with the ability that a photograph lacks to distinguish the essentials. He drew still lifes, nudes, and portraits in the same timeless, distilled style.

And yet they were far from flowing or automatic. Week after week, the same sitter or skull was lit in place, and, though the act of drawing would go on, you would sometimes wonder when it would *happen*. He made minimal progress from hour to hour, but never left his station. Watching Jacob draw was a bit like watching a climber on a sheer rockface, slowly trying out one crampon and then another, looking for a foothold, advancing a couple of feet and then spending the night on the rockface in his bag, upright—albeit a climber engaged in a steady conversation with a friend on the lost art of true rock climbing.

"I always wanted to be doing this," he said, meaning drawing in the classical style. "And I couldn't understand why the world wouldn't see it as legitimate. I drew from when I was really, really small—anything, comic books, Spider-Man. And then, when I started in art school, the attitude was 'That's great, so good, and, you know, pretty soon you'll outgrow this!' " He laughed. Jacob was always trying to strike a decent mean between affirmation of his secret faith that art had been going wrong since the 1860s and his desire not to get caught up in the reactionary grievance-keeping that disfigured much of the revivalist world he lived in. "You'll outgrow wanting to draw the world as it is, searching for this beauty, this place where light and the body meet—that was the attitude of most of the art teachers I had," he went on. "So I had to re-create a world in which I could do the kind of drawing I wanted to do. I wasn't alone in this. There were quite a few of us trying, and, bit by bit, and book by book, and practice by practice, we tried to remake the world of atelier realism that had been discarded and abandoned." Over time, he assembled a group of teachers and students and enthusiasts, all given over to the practice of classical drawing from life and plaster casts, and from that nucleus came this studio and then the Grand Central Academy.

As in any marginal community, there were, I learned, fierce schisms and expulsions. I say marginal; it was marginal to me, but it wasn't marginal to the people in it. Microworlds don't look micro to the microbes. (And what we think are macroworlds don't look macro to the next biggest thing up; Apollo smiles down from Parnassus on career retrospectives at MoMA.) Like all subcultures, this was a complete society, with rules and rivalries. Jacob referred disdainfully to "Tomming realists," by which

he meant realist artists who bowed and scraped before the masters of the avant-garde plantation, apologizing for their practice
and just asking for the freedom to hoe a few acres of representa-
tional oats. Jacob was a Jacobin: he didn't want his own humble
back forty to farm; he wanted the keys to the plantation house.

Sometimes we would talk about our kids, and sometimes
about music—he loved to play Bellini and Verdi in the studio,
and was trying to master string trios with his son and daughter. It was only when we talked about art that we disagreed: he
hated the triumph of modernism, and I did not, and there were
moments when I felt a bit like a lapsed Roman Catholic who, out
looking for a good Unitarian to show him a new spiritual path,
has found instead a cheerful, welcoming Satanist, though one
with a black Lab and kids at the same school. Jacob wanted to
rid his language of any taint of the age of the avant-garde. "I
don't even know what to call what I do," he said. "'Realism' is the
obvious name, but realism is a specific thing from modern art, all
that Courbet-derived stuff, meaning the primacy of belonging
to the world out there, and being accepted as an agitator. It's sort
of the *opposite* of what I'm after. 'Traditionalism' is OK, because
it's based on lost traditions, but that makes it sound too much
like just repeating something older. Neo-traditionalist? How
can something traditional be neo?" The best half-serious label
he could find was "traditional realist revivalism," and he had to
admit that it still wasn't very good. He knew that you couldn't
erase history; on the other hand, what if history was all wrong?
"You can't go back," he said once, sighing. "I know that. But you
can *look* back."

Over the weeks of listening and watching, I began at
last to draw the thing in front of me, or to try to. Jacob had
made one adjustment in what might generously be called my

"technique." Instead of holding the pencil tight and stabbing away, I was to hold it underhand, and make large sweeping, fencing-like gestures that might block out the general shape of whatever it was we were looking at. And then he told me to place an imaginary clock face on top of those first broad, easy underhand gestures.

"Just make tilts in time," he said. "Imagine that there's a clock overlaying what you're drawing. Then make one tilt on the clock, then check to see if it matches up with what you see, look to see if it's at the proper angle on the clock face, and then correct it. Make it the right time. Now, there, you've got that line"—a descending scrawl meant to indicate the upper slope of a skull we were drawing—"and it's at, oh, what would you say, twelve ten? I mean in relation to the vertical axis."

He stepped back and looked at my easel. "I would argue that, if you look at it again, the time on this clock is really much closer to twelve eleven, or twelve twelve . . ." He trailed off and looked fiercely at the page.

"Twelve thirteen?" I said, not wanting to seem completely blind.

"Yeah! Maybe you're right. Twelve thirteen." Then he said, formally, "That's an inquiry I'd like to pursue," and erased my line and let me add another, two degrees lower.

Nothing had prepared me for how one could fix a line merely by rubbing it out and implanting another line a bare thirty-second of an inch above or below. The choice of the first line could be freely made, unbounded, improvisational. For you could always erase and remake; the eraser was the best friend a would-be artist had. And the erased line, still barely visible beneath, had an eloquence of its own, since it smudged the space in a way that suggested pentimenti, second thoughts, a hazy penumbra of light and shadow. Light leaks into the world, and an erased line with a line above suggests that leakage. Nothing in a graduate degree in art history prepares you for the eloquence of the eraser.

I looked again at the erased space and the new scrawl. To my shock, it did have the faintest impress of anatomy, of organic life, of the way a jaw actually joins a skull.

"Yeah," Jacob said, nodding, as he looked at the new lean of the line, touching my shoulder as though my pencil had somehow just spat out a Raphael cartoon. He cheered up and went back to his own easel. "Now, don't worry about, you know, drawing or *art*. Just draw that clock hand in your head, one contour meeting the next, and ask, What time is it between them?" And so for hours, weeks, that's what I tried to do. I wasn't really drawing. But at least I was making tilts in time.

———

YOU CAN'T GO BACK, but you can look back, Jacob had said, and certainly he looked, and saw, for himself. We went to a show of Bronzino drawings at the Met, and I expected him to be impressed. Who was a greater master of classical drawing than Bronzino?

But Jacob was struck by how quickly Bronzino had settled on his solutions. "Well, now, he has this kind of model in his head, a formula. He sees a child and he sees these orbs." He gestured. "Three of them. Three balls, intersecting like pawnbrokers' balls: chubby legs, chubby chest, chubby head, and *boom*—a cherub." He made three quick circles with his right hand, and the typical form of a Bronzino cherub was written briefly in the air. "Do you notice how he has so much mastery of certain areas, and then he has the solution to others ready in his head?" He looked harder at the face of a Madonna and sighed. "There's a smoothness, a slightly comic-book-complacent solution, to his chins and ears."

We walked on and scrutinized a couple of well-muscled torsos. "You know, you can tell when someone's really *looking* at a body by the absence of parallel dents. When a person is standing or resting, the dent on one side of the body is usually met by a fullness on the other. When you get these two dents"—he pointed to what he meant—"it looks sort of stylish, but it's not really true, and you sense that. You rarely get a model whose rib cage is so clearly articulated and whole."

Looking at these beautiful drawings, I now realized that they were not found visions, or lines of poetry: they were made of tacit compromises between agreed-on fictions and hard-sought facts. Bronzino was called a mannerist not because that was where he happened to fall in the metaphysical chess game called "art history" but because he really had a manner. It was made of double dents and triple cherubic circles. Some fight between the ideal and the real, far from being a Neoplatonic abstraction, was actually going on in each drawing: when it tipped too far toward the ideal, it became a cartoon and lifeless; tip it too narrowly toward the actual, and it lost all the poetic sweep of the Grand Manner. The more you instructed yourself about the risks—the tussle of sight and muscle and bone—the more you appreciated the triumphs. The thing itself was argued out inch by inch on the page, not a foot or two above or just beside it, on the label.

We came at last to a small, unspectacular drawing of an old man. "I think this is the best drawing here," Jacob said. "Look how he's worried his way through that head, through the wrinkles—he's looking all the time in this one, and not letting his hand do the thinking for him."

At the end of the show, we stepped back out into the hall of the Met. "I can't say I'm too impressed by old Bronzino," Jacob said. "There aren't a lot of great drawings in there."

There was a mix-and-match show of Met drawings and prints on the way to the stairs, and we looked at an Alex Katz. Jacob made a face. It did look smooth, generalized, conceptualized, and simplified to the point of vacuity. Of course, I told myself, that was the point—to be smooth, stenographic, and direct—but for the moment I luxuriated in the originality of a shocked response.

"The *suckiness* of it," Jacob said. "I want my drawing not to suck." He was goading me, just a little, I knew, with a half-smile somewhere six levels down.

"It's a style," I said. "Deliberately smooth and simple."

"Simple, sure, because who needs good?" he teased. We inched toward an Andrea Mantegna, a bizarre engraving from the early 1470s of Silenus, the hideous and yet entrancing fat man. Jacob stopped.

"That is *great!*" he murmured. "I used to keep a Mantegna up in the studio just for hope. I mean, look at that." I knew the Mantegna was great, but, for the first time, I thought I saw *why* it was great: the discipline of drawing in play with an instinctive feeling for form, an unwillingness to compromise on what a fat, drunken old oracle would look like—those rolls on his thighs, the three chins, not neat orbs of cherub-chubbiness but real human lard—intermeshed with the dignity of myth. My hand tingled at the thought of trying to draw that way. I had always loved Mantegna, liked Alex Katz, enjoyed Bronzino; but now I understood that the intuitions had arguments, that the feelings were matched by facts. A drawing was a surface of minute claims and compromises and clichés—some places where the received or even idealized wisdom was accepted and some places where it was argued out and a new truth arrived at.

We stopped for coffee afterward, and I asked Jacob why, given his skill at seeing and showing the world as it was, he never wanted to draw the particulars of *this* world as it is, the world that we found ourselves in, where people met at endless dinner parties. He drew his kids, beautifully, but without their AirPods and iPhones and Vitaminwaters. Why not draw as a novelist might write, with the appurtenances and accessories of this time?

He looked at me and seemed almost angry. "No, that's— you've so absorbed the premises of modern realism into your head that you can't see past it. Why didn't Michelangelo draw people buying fish, instead of nudes and gods? He was looking for some idea of beauty, rooted in this world"—he made a gesture around the coffee shop, taking in everything, light and time and the human forms seated there—"that didn't need an iPhone to justify it. He really had an idea of timeless beauty. Why is beauty less interesting to you than journalism?"

Although I found the certainty of Jacob's exclusions odd, they had their resonance. I had come to feel not just inadequate as an art critic, in the absence of any skill, but also alienated from art in its current guise. Learning to draw was my way of confronting my disillusion with some of the louder sonorities and certitudes of the art with which I had grown up and for which I had once been a fierce advocate. For, surely, if there was absurdity in writing about art without being able to draw, there was even more comedy in valuing craft and praising mere cunning—in finding yourself trying to write skillfully about the purposefully skill-less. I could recite by heart the catechism: art had in the past century emancipated itself from mere description and cultivated an expertise less artisanal but no less demanding—conceptual, historically conscious, made of mind and thought. Over the years, however, the absence of true skill—the skill to do something with your fingers at the command of your mind, which can be done only by a few, after long practice—unmanned my love, and that created a problem for me. I could parse, and praise, a Jeff Koons fabrication or a Bruce Nauman video, but was I really in love with things so remote from the ancient daily struggle to make something look like something else? Someone out of sorts with the practice of an art form can still be a critic; someone out of sorts with the premise of an art form is merely a scold. A jazz critic who does not like improvisation does not like jazz. Yet I was still happiest in museums and thought I might remember why by learning to draw.

The funny thing was that Jacob knew the catechism too. I had been shocked to discover that a portrait that hung near his easel was of Meyer Schapiro, one of a handful of art historians who had invented the humanist appreciation of abstract art, and, it turned out, Jacob's great-uncle. Jacob knew the score. But what if he was right, and the whole thing had been a mistake, and we all had to start over from scratch, or at least from a sketch? It was a possibility worth looking at.

Later that week in the studio, there was a nude model, a perfectly muscled young man named Nate. Jacob made another correction in my drawing. He had me hold the pencil underhand again, and start by making sweeping, open guesses at the form, and then looking at the imaginary clock, erasing the off lines, correcting, making tilts in time.

But as I stared into the impossible landscape of ripples and nubs and shadows in Nate's torso, Jacob said, "Look into his torso and find a new form, another shape to draw. Something outside your symbol set."

I looked puzzled, and he explained, "I mean, don't draw a chest, or what you think a chest looks like. The ideas you've got in your head about the way things look—get rid of them. Find something else in there to draw. Find a dog. The outline of some small African nation. A face." He came around to hover over my shoulder. "See there, right in the space beneath his breastbone, I see this kind of snooty-looking butler, his chin pointing out and his nose in the air and his eyes half shut. Do you see him?" I squinted and looked, and then I did. Sort of: a face implicit in the accidents of light and shadow and flesh.

"OK. Just draw the butler with the side of your pencil, shade by shade, and you'll be drawing him." He gestured toward Nate. "Draw the snooty butler, and you'll start a solid passage."

I learned to burrow in, underhand, eraser at the ready, searching for swelled-up bullfrogs and smiling bats and butlers with their noses in the air and all the other odd shapes that the play of light on flesh produced. The way out was, homeopathically, the way back in: lose your schematic conventions by finding some surprising symbol or shape in the welter of shades, and draw that. Here was the brain's natural language of representation, as Leonardo knew, when he counselled artists, in the first true break toward life drawing, to look at the patterns of moss on cave walls and visualize clouds.

The ultimate kitsch representation of art-making is the moment in the movie *The Agony and the Ecstasy*, when Charlton Heston's Michelangelo, desperate to break his symbol set of divine likenesses, sees the nebulous form of God creating Adam in the clouds above his head. Now I saw that this scoffed-at scene is a purely pragmatic image of creativity: Michelangelo needed to break through his symbol set by finding new shapes to look at. Searching in the clouds for figures is the most rational course for an avid and alert artist to follow. We can't know if he saw his ceiling in the clouds, but he may have squinted and tried to see clouds, or butlers, in his ceiling.

———

WHY DO LIFE DRAWINGS look like life? Why do these collections of shrewdly borrowed shapes and broken lines strike us as real? After all, what is presented to our retina when we look at the bleached skull or the five and a half feet of naked person—the particular riot of color and light reflections, pink and white and dark—looks nothing like the six inches of orderly silver-to-black line marks on ivory paper. Even line itself, the assertion of a contour, however nuanced and optical the shadings within, is as fictional as a quotation mark. The process, as the Bronzino drawings showed, must involve some play of the "conceptual" (the shapes we know) and the "perceptual" (the shades we see). But how?

One view, which lingers in the social sciences, though it was long ago discarded in psychology, is that the language of line drawing is all conceptual, as artificial and in need of being learned as the Egyptian hieroglyphs. Yet every honest observer senses that a life drawing, no matter how many pawnbrokers' balls and snooty butlers it includes, has an edge of persuasive illusion. My drawings of Nate didn't look like Nate because that's what drawings of Nate look like. They looked like Nate because, however ineptly, they showed something of the way Nate looked.

Drawing has conventions, though. What counts as convincing now isn't the same as what counted as convincing in medieval times. In the twentieth century, in one of the most important books ever written about representation—Kenneth Clark called it "the most brilliant book of art criticism I have ever read"—E. H. Gombrich argued that in drawings, conventions always interact with perceptual information: "schemas," conventional symbolic images, come first, and then we correct them bit by bit as we observe and adjust them to life.

Gombrich's schemas are an art-historical version of the cognitive prosthesis of the Turk, a way of letting an artist take shortcuts to perfect sight. By using schemas, we shortcut the necessity of open-ended observation, of exactly the kind I had experienced in that first baffling visit to the Grand Central Atelier. Some of the schemas may be shorthand ways of organizing space and figures in advance of sight. Linear perspective is that kind of thing. Jacob's "tilts in time" were another good instance of a schema. Having only a reductive relationship to "recording what one sees," the schemata focus the artist on a controllable element, a minimalist step that, like perspective, can be neatly mechanized. From that mechanical armature, no more than an imaginary clock face imposed on the world, corrections and redrawings and amendments can be made, until the thing drawn begins to look like the world seen.

Most psychologists of art, and those historians of art who take an interest in its perceptual psychology, accepted that picture. But it now seems possible that tonal drawing is not the end result of an incremental process of pictorial probing and art historical progress. It may be the mind's first draft! In the 1970s, cognitive psychologist David Marr formalized the idea that, in effect, we see the real world first as a series of life drawings, as a shaded play of light falling on the world—what he called, half-jokingly, a "two-and-a-half-dimensional sketch," a field of cells that represents information about a surface or an edge.

Yet those mental sketches are of no use unless they're corralled by higher-level frames into discrete, fixed shapes—into exactly the "symbol set" that Jacob was trying to get me to discard. Some of those frames help to orient us in space, distinguish up from down and left from right, but some are more richly symbolic: they help us sort out recurring forms from mere incidents of light. We turn shades into shapes, and then shapes into symbols.

The new view is that our Western life-drawing tradition is a neat bit of cognitive jujitsu; the sophisticated "optical" rendering of generalized regions and nuanced shade actually represents the more "primitive" mental map. It took Leonardo and Raphael to show us what the mind's eye sees first—regions and shadings, instead of conceptual shapes and things—while every cartoonist shows us what it sees second. In fact, the new idea suggests that life drawing is less an acquired instrument of slow-crawling craft and more just something back there that we delve deep to find again. This may in turn help explain the enduring mystery of why the oldest of all human representations, the cave paintings of Altamira, Lascaux, and Chauvet, are expertly rendered as shaded, three-dimensional life drawings, full of persuasive highlight and shadow. The caveman in us still draws what he sees, until the Egyptian in us interferes. (Certain language-disabled kids can make drawings that seem precociously optical, and, where people used to claim that the emergence of art is proof of symbolic, language-based culture, psychologist Nicholas Humphrey has argued that the existence of the perfectly modulated cave paintings suggests that the people who made them didn't yet know how to talk.)

Yet the "symbolic frames" that organize our representation of vision don't seem to be hardwired; they change all the time. We can learn to draw from life, but we can also learn to understand those abstract funny faces with their movable eyebrows. This is why, though what visual psychology can say about drawing is rich, what it can say about art is limited. Symbolic games aren't set. The seeing mind, or the drawing hand, is like a dealer in a poker game, who, as the players get bored with five-card draw or seven-card stud, calls out a new variant: now lowest hand triumphs; now deuces are wild; now the highest hand and the lowest hand both can take the pot. A cartoonish Philip Guston scrawl or a slick John Currin contour can both be winners.

Drawing is one of those things that sit on the uneasy and bending line between instinct and instruction, where seeming perversity eventually trumps pleasure as the card players and the kibitzers interact and new thrills are sought. And this truth was the source of Jacob's discontent. His real dream, I saw, was to drive the kibitzers from the temple of card playing, as mine was to become a card player, not a kibitzer. But in truth, kibitzers and card players, observers and artists, shades and shapes and symbols are all parts of a single game, shuffled together in the big bluff we call culture. Without the card players, as Jacob knew, there was no skill in the game, but without the kibitzers, there was no skin in it, no point to watching. In fact, without the kibitzers you couldn't even call the activity a game, more just an obsession—which, at times, is what it seemed to be for Jacob, and for me.

For a few months, I had been searching for strange shapes to break my symbol set. One day, when Nate was posing, I began to make quick stabs, and sketches. I saw a kind of hamster with soft rabbit ears where his shoulder joined his arm, its blunt snout pressing toward the eyes, and I tentatively drew that. I was following the image, doing sight-system checking, sketching the animal shapes, making tilts in time, rubbing out the weaker lines and letting the better ones bloom . . . and, miraculously, the

outline of an arm appeared, and a shoulder, and it all looked more
or less right.

It was a terrible drawing, I knew, but it was not a conceptual
schema, a mere cognitive prosthesis, of an arm and shoulder. It
was some recognizable rendering of the pattern of light in front
of me. Jacob came over and said, "Yeah, that's got some of the
shape. I would argue that you could erase here just slightly." It
was, as I say, a terrible drawing—the core was way too wide,
so that I had given Nate a Herculean expanse of torso, way out
of proportion to the arms—but the relation between arm and
shoulder was almost human, almost recognizably true. It was the
best thing I had ever drawn, and I realized that I hadn't drawn it
as I had imagined, God's hand finally resting on mine to steal a
true contour from the world. No, I had made it up out of small,
stale parts and constant reapplications of energy and observation,
back and forth. I stood back. The good bit was about two and a
half inches long, and no good at all by any standard. But it was a
stab at a shape seen, at a pattern of incoming light and shade that
made a shape. I was drawing.

The rhythm of fragment and frustration, of erasure and error
and slow emergence of form, was familiar. I'd hoped that drawing would be an experience of resistance and sudden yielding,
like the first time you make love, where first it's strange and then
it's great, and afterward always in some way the same. Instead,
drawing foreshadowed every other skill I'd acquire and recapitu-
lated the simpler ones I'd already achieved in life: skating, guitar
playing, sauce-making. Sauce-making! Life drawing was like my
mother's lesson in making beef Stroganoff. You took one seemingly unrelated and in itself unappetizing step, sautéing peppers
or adding sour cream to tomato paste, and the totality of the effect
only emerged when everything came together. "Delicious" is a

sub-function of discrete actions. Ugly bits slowly built up, discouragingly not at all like what you want, until it is.

The bad news, I was finding out, was that life drawing was just like everything else you learned to do, a slow carpentering of fragments into the illusion of a harmonious whole. The good news was that drawing was like everything else, and even I could learn to do it.

———

THERE WAS ONE missing piece left to discover, though. One Friday I went to the studio to draw, and there was a naked woman there. We had been drawing Nate, and Nate was fine—but Anna was *gorgeous*, redheaded and voluptuous, and I swallowed hard as I set out to stare at her and find a frog or a snooty butler or a newly independent African nation in the burrows and hollows of her body.

"Hi," she said when I came in. She looked bored beyond words, though she chewed gum with a thoughtful, rhythmic grace. I had just come back from a parent-teacher conference, and Jacob and I talked briefly about fifth-grade curricula.

"Our kids go to the same school," I called out to Anna, who was posing under the hot spotlight. She moved her red hair away from her face and readjusted her torso.

"Yeah, so I gather," she said. She had an old-fashioned, Seventh Avenue accent.

I stared between her breasts innocently, virtuously—and found, at last, a spaniel on its back, its paws in the air. (My kids had just got a dog.) I began to touch and erase and touch again, and Anna's body took shape under my pencil. Jacob came over and corrected my drawing. I had mismeasured the proportions between breast and pubis. "Measurement is so essential," he said.

He explained that we always make heads and hands oversized, and fill in the middle, as though the places of maximum sensory attention naturally demand the most attention. But I still couldn't get the proportions of Anna's torso right. So, as Jacob had taught me, I held my hands up in a small square to adjust the "sight-size"—making both the thing seen and the thing drawn fit into the same square—and then, in frustration, held a thumb out and squinted with one eye so that I could have an easier measure of the distance, as I saw it. Hands in small square, thumb out, and squinting—my God, I was acting like every artist in every silent movie I had ever seen!

Jacob came over and looked at my nude. "You've got this too far down." He pointed to the light-gray haze I meant for her pubic triangle. It should have been much higher up. I erased and began to adjust. "You've centered it, because in your symbol set that's where it belongs. Look again." I moved the little triangular schema up and over.

"Her nipples, you've got them centered too," Jacob said. "They are at angles akimbo to each other. Look at the angle. Tell time." I pushed one nipple a smidge off center and left the other one alone, and then made the pubic triangle more like the bicycle-seat shape it really was. Suddenly, she was alive—right there on the page! I had a flick of desire for a mark I had just made on a page with a pencil. Appetite drives drawing; that's what makes sure that there is no such thing as abstract art. I stepped back. It was not just closer to the truth but sexy, real, my own paltry Galatea.

Anna came over and looked. She was obviously disappointed. It was still a pretty crappy drawing. But then I saw her as she was, which was neither as she was on the couch nor as she was on my paper. She was tiny. I am a small man, but she came up to my shoulder. There she was on the page, though, as voluptuously large as a Matisse model. Jacob laughed. "There's a fiction part of what we do too," he said. The truest drawing is the most feigning, and no help for it.

Jacob turned his drawing of Anna into a painting, and it is the centerpiece of his new exhibition at the Adelson Galleries. In the painting, she looks sultry, pained, a Rubens version of an Andrew Wyeth mistress. I can hear the art historians of the future speculating sapiently on her mood, her melancholy, even on her relation to the painter.

I stepped away from the studio after the year, though I still draw in private whenever I can. What had I learned? Accomplishment, and even mastery of Jacob's perverse and proud kind, was a composite of small steps. There is no straight line that you can draw around a circumstance to take its shape away; there are only marks, made underhand, tilts in time that you erase and adjust and erase again, over and over, until the black dog barks and the afternoon ends and you close your pad, and call it life.

Making Magic

O N   A   L O N G   P L A N E   R I D E   H O M E   T O   N E W   Y O R K
from Las Vegas, a man and a boy are playing with cards.
Only their hands are visible to the people sitting near them, so
that, as they shuffle and reshuffle and fan and deal, they seem to
be engaged in a game of gin rummy that never quite begins. The
hands move, first large and crabby, then small and soft, in example and imitation, and all through the night, hour after hour—
while everyone else on the plane sleeps or dozes or watches
DVDs on a laptop—their hands move and their voices murmur.

What they are doing is magic, and, because it is magic, it
requires hour upon hour of hard work. A magician is teaching
an apprentice how to do a card trick—a trick so complicated
and subtle that it will, when finally shown, be almost too subtle
to enjoy. It is called Twisting the Aces: the four aces are shown
facedown; they are counted out, still facedown, one by one; the
packet of cards is twisted, and each time the aces are counted
out, one of them, a different ace each time, appears faceup. It's as
though inside the packet the cards, untouched by human hands,
were somehow turning over.

The magician and his apprentice are believers in the deep and narrow art of closeup card magic. A few nights earlier, they had gone, with a dozen or so other people, on a rare late-night tour of the illusionist David Copperfield's warehouse, which contains the world's greatest collection of magic paraphernalia. All of Houdini's most important boxes—the Water Torture Cell, the Metamorphosis Trunk—were there, but the magician had walked over to a wall where a tiny book was kept under a false cover. "It's Malini's Erdnase!" he said, as one might say "It's Lincoln's Bible!" The magician's face came alive as he looked through it. The boy watched, rising up on his toes to gaze at the small old-fashioned engravings of hands, neatly turned with late-nineteenth-century cuffs, manipulating cards, hands and cards, hands and cards, page after page.

The boy is one of the tribe that you will find every Saturday afternoon at Tannen's Magic, a windowless shop on the sixth floor of a nondescript building on West Thirty-Fourth Street. All afternoon, the magic boys step into a tiny elevator that takes them to Tannen's. They are often searching for relief from a needle of worry in their minds. They go to buy tricks, "gaffs," that will lend them magic. An acute boy might sense that Tannen's once was greater, or at least bigger. On a back table, he can find, half-discarded in a big tub, faded old blueprints for illusion boxes—instructions for making magic cabinets of a kind that no one makes anymore. "Girl in a Dream: Illusion Plan No. 1223," one boy reads out to a friend as they decide to buy a plan as a memento of the old magic. (Actually, it's "Girl in a Drum," but they find out only when they get it home.)

The magic boys—and they are almost always boys, in need of the illusion of secret powers and obsessed by repetitive practices—often go for a Saturday meal to a Mexican restaurant around the corner, where they show each other their tricks. Some of them have heard of a better magicians' dinner in the back room of a little restaurant and sports bar off Ninth Avenue called the Joshua Tree. The gathering takes place in the small hours, after the last curtain of "Monday Night Magic," a lovely chamber session of magicians that has somehow survived for ten years in various theaters around the city. One of the luckiest things that has happened to me in New York is being able to go to the Joshua Tree and watch the magicians work and listen to them talk:

"That guy?" a murmured monologue might begin. "He had a bunch of details on the Revolve Vanish that both Ganson and Fulves kind of overlooked. See, Slydini always said 'stiff, then dead,' so when you show the coin, the hand is stiff, and then when you turn the hand it goes dead for an instant, like an intermediate beat, when the coin is released, but then also you don't move your hand forward on its own. The thing Tony taught is that you move the torso forward, and that it turn carries the arm forward and therefore the hand. So, that—that's the real work on that."

And on and on like that, in dreamlike composite. Magicians, as I've said, have the most rapturous and absorbed shoptalk of any artists I know. This is partly because magicians have leisure between gigs, and partly because much of the pleasure of being a magician is membership in a subculture, where methods and myths can be appreciated only by initiates. Magicians are, in their relations with one another, both extremely generous and extremely jealous. Just as chefs know that recipes are of little value in themselves, magicians know that learning the method is only the beginning of doing the trick—a baby step toward the real work.

If I had to choose one moment where I have sensed myself in the aura of the real work, pure and clear, it might be the night I watched Jamy Ian Swiss, over dinner at the Joshua Tree, perform thirteen versions of the pass in about as many seconds. The pass (it is sometimes called "the shift," and card cheaters call one version "the hop") is among the glories of advanced sleight of hand. Diagrammed by S. W. Erdnase in *The Expert at the Card Table*, a treatise he published in 1902, it involves moving a packet of cards invisibly from the center of the deck to the top. Judging the quality of any magician's pass is inherently difficult, since the better it is done the harder it is to see that anything has happened. To watch Jamy Ian Swiss perform thirteen versions of the pass is to see this: The cards in his hand, then one card—say, the three of clubs—inserted somewhere, anywhere, in the middle of the deck. His hands burp and hiccup for half a second, merely squaring the deck, and then the three of clubs is disclosed, right back on top. He runs through a number of variants: the riffle pass, the stroboscopic pass, the dribble pass . . . The other magicians nod, knowingly, like bird-watchers seeing an unusual find in the middle distance.

Swiss is widely thought to have one of the masterly sleight-of-hand techniques in the world today, and the pass is one of his accomplishments. Seeing him do thirteen versions of it is therefore a little like seeing Yo-Yo Ma practice scales in rehearsal at Carnegie Hall. On the other hand, it is not at all like watching Yo-Yo Ma practice scales, since the audience is likely to include someone like Chuy, the Mexican Wolfman, an amiable sideshow artist with a very, very full beard, or the Great Throwdini, the knife thrower, and his target girl, Tina, not to mention Simon Lovell, an underfed, pale-green-and-white-complexioned Englishman who is a master card cheat—I have seen him make whole decks disappear and replace them with other decks in less time than it takes to describe it—and Todd Robbins, who is now perhaps the last remaining sideshow artist capable of doing the

Human Blockhead act (a six-inch steel nail goes into and up the nose) while giving a scholarly account of its origins.

The few civilians who do come around as often as not have no idea of the quality of what they're seeing—the magician's eternal plight being that of a Yo-Yo Ma, who, after he plays, has people come up onstage and tell him that they know how he does it, he scrapes that bow thing across the strings, and, anyway, they have an uncle who used to play the cello a little, some baroque thing, has he ever heard that number? Most cellists, in those circumstances, would do what most magicians do—nod politely and say yes, I bet your uncle was a real music lover, and retreat into beer and diffidence. Perhaps one cellist in a generation would say no, scraping a bow against a string has nothing to do with making music, you don't know how it's done, you actually have no *idea* how it's done, and your uncle was no more a cellist than a man with a hi-fi is a conductor.

Jamy Ian Swiss is that cellist. He is as absolute in his passions and prohibitions as a Zen master, albeit one with a Vandyke, a small potbelly, an earring in his left ear, and a taste for black-background Hawaiian shirts. Most nights, he maintains a note of conspiratorial mirth, leaning in toward a listener to share outrage over some stupidity—"Can you believe that guy!"—and breaking into a wolfish grin. But at times he lowers into a kind of set-faced gloom at the things the world is willing to watch and praise. Tender in his connections, a gentle and inspiring teacher of young magicians (he has performed a marriage ceremony for at least one, the closeup man Matthew Holtzclaw), he can be brutal in his beliefs. In an old-fashioned, barking Brooklyn accent, part Bogart hiss and part Art Carney howl, he produces at the table a flow of interrogations, exclamations, verdicts, and interdictions. "Magic only 'happens' in a spectator's mind," he puts it emphatically. "Everything else is a distraction. Magic talk on the Internet is a distraction. Magic contests are a distraction. Magic organizations are a distraction. The latest advertisement, the latest trick—distractions. Methods for their own sake are a distraction. You cannot cross over into the world of magic until you put everything else aside and behind you—including your own desires and needs—and focus on bringing an experience to the audience. This is magic. Nothing else." He is a master of the mystery of performance, of the way that misdirection is not merely a magician's tool but a kind of permanent principle of human psychology. We all "lap the track" on other people's expectations, readjust our performances to outwit our audience's anticipation, even if our audience is no larger than a dinner-table party listening to a joke. We see them anticipate the punch line and try to twist it before they can. Magicians know that the meta level of life, far from being a specialized place for ironists and philosophers, is the place where we live. We are always all outguessing each other's guesses, always trying to surprise someone else with what we've guessed they'd never guess and when they guess it, telling them, "Guess again!"

A producer and collector of practical aphorisms—"In every other art, technique must be transparent; only in magic must it be invisible"; "Don't run when they're not chasing you"; "Don't make unimportant things important"; "Magicians have taken something intrinsically profound and made it look trivial"; "Closeup magic is an art looking for an easel"—Swiss is perhaps the most feared (and resented) intellectual in the world of magic, with the saving ironic awareness that almost no one knows that there are in his world any intellects to be feared or resented. ("Mimes were invented to give magicians someone to look down on," he said one night.) He is a true intellectual in that he cannot help arguing about ideas even when it would be in his own interest, narrowly conceived, to stop. When someone says something stupid about magic, or sells something fake, or performs derivatively or cynically in some way, he just can't abide it—just cannot *accept* it—and uses whatever forum he has to denounce the offense. In regular columns in the magic magazines *Genii* and *Antinomy*, he launches impassioned assaults on phony magic, on "street magic," on Internet magic, and on any other kind of magical practice that seems to him to have brought shame on his profession.

The world at large, of course, is not particularly interested in hearing why someone is wrong about magic, or doing magic the wrong way—it's all most people can do to order up a magic show once a year for their kid's birthday—and the magicians Jamy thinks are wrong certainly don't want to hear it, and so, like all intellectuals, he probably exasperates as many people as he enlightens. There are those—especially on websites and among YouTube magicians—who believe that Jamy is a man out of time, defending a dying tradition in the face of a renaissance of new and edgier sorts of conjuring. Jamy writes to attack them, and they respond in kind. (Even his enemies call him Jamy. It's a small world.) People who don't like him find his relentless search for the meaning of magic tiresome or just pretentious. Those who follow and admire him find something gallant, and Cyrano-like, in his quest to make magic matter, not as a redoubt of nostalgia but as a living art that might cross over with the other arts. Yet even his triumphs are shaded by the rueful knowledge that often all he has to prove his convictions is card tricks, and the handful of people who care.

On the plane, Swiss's voice rises a touch: "You've got to—no, you've got to relax your wrist just then, you have to—you want it to look more casual. You're making too much of the moment. The ace is no big deal. Don't force it. Let it happen." The boy's hands go flat, and turn and start again.

———

MAGICIANS LIKE TO SAY that magic is as old as civilization, stretching back to Egyptian priests and Greek oracles. But stage magic, performed magic, in which conjuring is acknowledged as craft and entertainment—in which, in one of Swiss's favorite aphorisms, the honest magician promises to deceive you, and then does—is probably a few hundred years old. In his essay "A Millennium of Magic Literature," Swiss accepts the significance of the date 1584, when Reginald Scot's book *Discoverie of Witchcraft* and Jean Prevost's *Clever and Pleasant Inventions* were published. Scot and Prevost, he explains, write similar things, slightly at cross-purposes: Scot is "discovering," that is, debunking, witchcraft—there are no witches, he says, and he explains how the make-believe witches achieve apparently magical effects. Prevost's book presents itself as a book of tricks, to be done for pleasure. From the start, then, the history of magic-as-fun is interwoven with the history of magic-as-fraud, more or less the way the history of chemistry is bound up with the history of alchemy.

Modern magic may begin around 1905, in Ottawa, when the very young David Verner read Erdnase's *The Expert at the Card Table*. Appropriately, it's a deeply mysterious text. Who Erdnase was and why he wrote, and self-published, his book are two abiding enigmas of modern magic. No one of that name has ever been found, and the general agreement is that it is a pseudonym, probably for someone named Andrews. He seems to have been a card shark rather than a magician; most of the book is taken up with cheating techniques, daintily not always called such. (As for why he gave away his craft, William Kalush, the founder of the leading magic library in New York, suggests that Erdnase may have been suffering from the perpetual fantasy among nonwriters that writing books is a way to make money.) In Erdnase, you see the same relation between display and deceit that has always been part of magic, only instead of doing things that could get you burned alive at an auto-da-fé he is doing things that could get you shot dead at a card table. But his inventory of closeup skills—the cull, the break, the shift, the color change—became the foundation of twentieth-century closeup magic.

David Verner, or Dai Vernon, as he became onstage, is the protagonist of modern magic, the Jesus to Erdnase's John the Baptist. Improbable though it seems for a closeup card magician who spent much of his life in residence at a private magic club, he has been the subject of two full-scale biographies, one of them a multivolume scholarly work, not to mention a huge commemorative and annotative literature within the magic world. Trying to explain his stature to civilians, magicians call him "the Picasso of magic," but Vernon is really something closer to its Marcel Duchamp. Like Duchamp, he responded to the drying up of the natural niche for his art form in his lifetime not by trying to compete with the new media—with the revolution that the photographic image and movies had wrought—but by seceding from the outside world, making magic into a secretive coterie art rather than an expansive public one.

Vernon worked at a time when movie palaces were pushing out magic venues and theaters. The great illusionist shows were slowly going out of business, while closeup magic went on mostly in nightclubs. By the 1930s, as Vernon's biographer David Ben writes, "amateur magicians, with stars in their eyes, had little idea of how unsatisfying the work could be. Performers traveled great distances and performed numerous shows before unappreciative audiences. . . . Those who presented large-scale illusions, 'Tall Grass Showmen,' were shunted to the hinterlands and focused their efforts on the cities, towns and villages that received little entertainment—of any sort."

Throughout the '20s and '30s, Vernon alternated magic shows, some successful, with long periods as an itinerant silhouette cutter. Yet during this discouraging time for magic he began the work that led to his greatest routines, among them Twisting the Aces and Triumph, in which a deck mixed up faceup and facedown suddenly straightens itself out, producing, as a bonus, a selected card. Triumph is to magic what "I Got Rhythm" is to jazz, the basis of innumerable variations.

Two stories shape Vernon's myth. The first is about how, in Chicago in 1922, he fooled Houdini, who boasted of being able to figure out any card trick, with a version of the routine called the Ambitious Card. Vernon was put off by Houdini's bad grace in the face of his own perplexity, and this helped create a divide that can still be found among magicians: between those who see Houdini, perhaps the most famous name in entertainment history, as essentially a tourist trap—a Salvador Dalí, there for the flash and the obvious effects, but not even a competent closeup man or illusionist—and those who see Houdini's fame as proof positive that he did the first thing a magician needs to do, which is to grasp the mind of his time.

The second story is about how, in the 1930s, Vernon embarked on what became the legendary quest of modern magic, the search for the center dealer. (Karl Johnson tells the story beautifully in his book *The Magician and the Cardsharp*.) Vernon had heard rumors of a card shark who was able to deal not merely the bottom card or the second card of the deck, in the usual way, but from its center—meaning that a chosen card could be dealt at will, no matter where the deck was cut—and, after years of looking in the hardscrabble gamblers' underground of Depression America, he found him, just outside Kansas City. Vernon learned the move and taught it to a handful of other magicians.

The story, as usually told, emphasizes Vernon's search for "naturalness," for methods of card manipulation that would look entirely real, even under scrutiny. The deeper meaning of the myth, though, is that the magician is one of the few true artists left on Earth for whom the mastery of technique means more than anything that might be gained by it. He center-deals but makes no money—doesn't even win prestige points—because *nobody knows he's doing it*.

Vernon grasped that there is an imbalance between the spectator's experience and the performer's, greater even than the normal imbalance in the arts between the insider and the outsider. We could watch Horowitz's fingers on the keyboard as we listened to the music; if we could admire Vernon's fingers on the deck as he did the trick, he wouldn't be doing it right. This makes insiders' experience of magic distinctive, a clinging together within a charmed circle of knowledge. Erdnase's genuine criminality became, in Vernon's hands, a kind of symbolic criminality—an aesthetic of the clandestine.

Vernon's insistence on "natural handling," on making every move look casual rather than "presentational"—like a man handling cards rather than like a magician handling props—is a precept of modern magic. But magic, like novel writing or acting, is *always* bending toward naturalism, and, very quickly, the forms of naturalism become rigidly stylized. The nineteenth-century magician Robert-Houdin insisted on magicians' wearing gentle-man's evening clothes, instead of the elaborate sorcerer's and Chinese costumes that conjurers usually wore onstage. The white tie and tails and top hat became the magician's regalia well into the twentieth century, long after everyone else had stopped wearing them. Like the Polish Hasidim, whose move toward spontaneous religion kept them in the ordinary clothes of the eighteenth century, magicians wore a costume that had first been meant as camouflage. The task of making magic seem natural must be perpetually renewed, and is more complex than just making it look offhand.

One night a year ago, a young magician came into the Joshua Tree and auditioned while Swiss sat having grilled salmon and a microbrew. He did a "torn and restored" bill trick—tearing up a dollar bill and then making it whole again. Swiss took him aside, and could be seen talking to him, sharply but intensely, explaining, teaching. Someone asked what was wrong with the trick; it had seemed very neatly done.

"He *was* appealing—he did have a nice persona," Swiss said, leaning into the table. "He could do the moves. But he tore the dollar up slowly, like this." Swiss replicated the young magician's careful, studied action. "Why? Why would you tear it up slowly? Nobody tears a dollar bill up in the first place, but, if you're going to tear up a dollar bill at all, you'd tear it up quickly, in a sudden fit, zip-zip-zip." He demonstrated. "The only reason you would tear a dollar bill up slowly is if you were doing something else to it at the same time—if you were doing a goddamn magic trick. So right away we're off in the magic land of 'I have in my hand an ordinary deck of cards.' But, OK, let's live with that. Why are you tearing it up? Are you doing it angrily? Gaily? Why are you asking me to watch you tear up a dollar bill? The method is not the trick. The method is never the trick. Once you've mastered the method, you've hardly *begun* the trick."

The method is never the trick. It is another way of saying that the method of life drawing, the marks made in obedience to the pattern of light, is not what brings life to the drawing, or that the chess-playing efficacy of the Turk was more than the moves its manipulator made from his hiding place. "Naturalism," "persuasive illusion," even "a cool card trick" are not neatly notched events on a stick of achievement, predictably progressing, like a child's growth registered on the bedroom wall. They instead are constantly in play within the movement of our minds. As our expectations become more hardened and our perceptions more acute, as our minds become habituated to one kind of performance or display, we are no longer persuaded or impressed or entrapped when we recognize it, and the artist or magician or chess master has to seek out some new effect or display or pattern—usually involving *not* doing exactly the thing that was impressively done in the last generation, or even a moment ago.

That is why life drawing, however passionately Jacob believed in the one right solution—absolute truth to the play of light on objects!—still has a history and is still visible to us as a series of period styles, even as we respect the craft tradition the styles may share. It's why the persuasive manifestation of "naturalism" in magic is one day dressed up in a tuxedo and the next in jeans and a T-shirt. Arts large and small, major and minor, are always on a constantly turning wheel of invention. One generation's "Such irony!" is the next generation's "So obvious!" What makes a great magic trick is not skill alone, nor even performance alone, but skill and performance placed within a story that stays one neat step ahead of the audience's expectations. (Trail too far behind and what you do is merely corny; leap too far ahead and it is avant-garde. They catch up eventually, but, as a working arti-san, you may starve in the meanwhile. We make such starving, far-ahead artists saints in some parts of our cultural domain, but there's no guarantee sainthood will happen, and when it does, it happens too late to be of help.)

There can never be a timeless "good card trick," because each trick is part of a history of expectations and surprise, its power changing as they do. In the same way, there can never be a "sci-ence of stories," since exactly what makes each story matter is its difference from the story just heard before. Nor any art without a history. We are all trying to figure out the trick; having figured it out, a new trick emerges.

———

ALL GROWN-UP CRAFT depends on sustaining a frozen moment from childhood: scientists, it's said, are forever four years old, wide-eyed and self-centered; writers are forever eight, over-aware and indignant. The magician is a permanent pre-adolescent. At least, all lives of magicians begin with a twelve-year-old at a place like Tannen's. "Jamy Ian Swiss is actually my name," Jamy said at another dinner. "And I grew up in Brooklyn, in Flatbush and then in Sheepshead Bay. My mother gave those names to me because 'Jamy' couldn't be shortened, and 'Ian' sounded elegant and English somehow, high-class. The 'Swiss' is a Jewish name that got changed somewhere along the road." Often battling with his mother, he loved his father, who got him started in magic. "I was an awkward and shy kid, with bottle-glasses and a horrific speech impediment," he said. "Then one day my father brought home, to amuse me, a Color Vision box that he had bought at Tannen's."

The Color Vision box is one of the simplest of self-working

tricks. The magician gives you a cube with a different color on each side and a box; you put the cube in the box with the color of your choice facing up and replace the lid. The magician discerns your choice without seeming to open the box. "I thought it was wonderful, amazing, and he taught me how to do it," Swiss said. "And then we started going to Tannen's together, taking the train in on Saturdays, all the way from Sheepshead Bay to Times Square.

"In those days, Tannen's was in the Wurlitzer Building, behind Bryant Park, where the Verizon Building is now. You just can't imagine the effect Tannen's could have in those days on a shy kid with a speech impediment. It was a scene! Everyone would be there! There were photographs of magicians from floor to ceiling, and shadow boxes filled with effects, and Tannen's symbol, a hat and a rabbit, was inlaid right in the linoleum. And so full of light! The magicians were everywhere, and they were such elegant and resourceful men. They would all drop in and do work just for the pleasure of it. Lou Tannen himself was there, a kind man who loved magic and sympathized with kids. He actually taught me a version of the cups and balls. Whenever anyone asks me how I started, I say, 'Just the same way you did. When I was awkward and twelve and bought a trick.'"

It was around then that Swiss had his first epiphany about the power of magic and its risks. "We had a mixed-up family, often at odds with each other, but there was one cousin, I'll call her Sharon, whom I adored. I would show her the Color Vision box, over and over, and she *loved* me for doing it. She couldn't get enough of it. But she kept begging me and begging me to show her how I did it, and at last I did. And she was furious—absolutely furious! The trick was so simple, even stupid. I learned a huge lesson that day, and not just not to tell civilians the secrets. It was more complicated and ambiguous than that, and it's taken me years to work out all of its meanings. It was"—he paused—"it was that the trick was not the trick, and that it was the interchange between us that was the source of the effect."

At the age of twenty-nine, after short flings in the pet trade and the telephone business, Swiss took a year off, while his wife at the time supported him, and spent it doing nothing but sleight of hand. "Mastering magic at twenty-nine is as late to begin seriously as it would be if you were studying violin. I felt that I had hands like stumps. It's why I still so envy closeup men like Prakash, who has such soft hands. By the end of the year, I had begun to get very good, technically, and I had heard somewhere that you could work as a magic bartender. So I went to bartender school." He looked across the table. "I loved being a bartender. Loved it! There was a blue-collar side to it, I suppose. I didn't talk with an accent like this, growing up. It was a rebellion against my cosseted middle-class upbringing. Magic was for me partly an art thing, partly a blue-collar artisanal thing, so being a magic bartender was ideal." He barks his bark. "Ha! It turned out that the whole idea of magic bars was dying even as I entered it."

In 1985, Swiss went to see a magician-and-juggler act he had been hearing about for a couple of years, called Penn & Teller. They were in the middle of their legendary stand at the Westside Arts Theatre. "The night shook me up completely. I mean, beyond completely! They made fun of magicians, and still did brilliant magic. And they refused to say that they were magicians doing a magic show, although that was obviously what it was."

Two years later, Swiss went to work at the Magic Castle, the famous club in Hollywood. "I was arrogant enough to call the Castle and say that I was free to lecture or perform," he says, shaking his head, "and they let me do some work there.

Naturally, I was desperate to see Vernon, and we sessioned together." Sessioning is the magicians' equivalent of jamming. Dai Vernon, who died in 1992, just shy of a century, had been the magician-in-residence there since the late sixties. "I can still recall everything he did. I did some things for him, one of them a slow-motion coin-vanish routine. That Friday, I did the afternoon lunch shows in the Close-up Gallery. Two shows. When I walked out for the first show, there was Vernon sitting in the front row, a little to my right. He was mere feet from me, and my hands began to shake. I almost dropped a gaff. Afterward, I came out and saw Vernon at the bar. I approached and apologized for my shakiness. 'You scared the hell out of me.' He waved me off.

"When I entered for the second show, there he was again, much to my surprise. I was calmer this time and the show came off without a hitch." On Sunday, Swiss gave a lecture and Vernon was there again: "I asked Vernon, 'So, Professor, did you see anything you liked?' He said, 'What do you mean, did I see anything I liked? I stayed awake for the whole thing, didn't I?'"

On the plane, the hands move. "Now, this is called Twisting the Aces," the boy explains to his father, who has put down his book, curious. "It's a Vernon trick, isn't it?" the boy asks the magician. He nods. The boy keeps a picture of Vernon as the screen saver on his computer, still young and dapper, cigarette in hand, all smoke and cards.

The boy's hands move, trying to conceal something.

"Make it natural, make it easy," the magician says.

Swiss befriended Penn and Teller, and began working with them on illusions, ideas, and routines. ("Penn taught me to drive. I'm a New Yorker, you know. Who drives? Penn put me in a car and said, 'My ability to speak quickly and clearly is the only thing keeping us alive.'") But his friendship with Vernon led him in another direction as well—backward, in a sense, to try to define what it was that made magic matter, why the tradition counted, and what it meant. He began to think about magic as an entertaining form of skepticism rather than as a debased form of mysticism.

In one way, this was de rigueur for magicians. Houdini had unmasked psychics. But it challenged the way Swiss understood his own work. A lot of magicians saw stage and closeup magic simply as fake "wonder," reproducing, in admittedly artificial ways, old rituals of death and restoration, giving people the hope, for half an hour, that real magic was possible. Even Edmund Wilson, an amateur magician, insisted that magic's most enduring effects came from its imitation of ancient mystery religion. Vernon, though, knew better. As he put it, "A spectator never or rarely was fooled by what a magician performed for him in the way of tricks."

As Swiss wrote the series of essays that were eventually collected in his book *Shattering Illusions*, he arrived at the idea that magic was, in his words, "an experiment in empathy"—a contest of minds, in which the magician dominates by a superior grasp of the way minds work. The spectator is not a dupe who gets fooled but a rational actor who gets outreasoned. When the aces are twisted, the viewer doesn't think, That's supernatural! The viewer thinks, I know it's a trick, but my mind is unable to imagine how any trick of the fingers could alter the cards when they're obviously still right in the middle of the pack.

In a recent summing-up essay in *Antinomy*, Swiss observed that, whereas a juggler like the young Penn Jillette doesn't have to imagine an audience to experience his effects, the magician must: "From the very start, the moment a magician looks into his practice mirror, he is envisioning an alien awareness—a mind other than his own, perceiving an illusion that he is creating but cannot actually experience for himself." Only by a command of intellectual empathy can the magician lead the viewer down an explanatory highway from which there is no exit, or, better, from which there are six exits, all of them blocked. Magic is imagination working together with dexterity to persuade experience how limited its experience really is, the heart working with the fingers to remind the head how little it knows.

"The one thing I can do that Steven Spielberg can't is to say, 'Take a card, any card you like,'" Swiss says. "And I can have you sign it, so that it's unique in the world, and then I can make it disappear from the deck and find it in your pocket and hand it back to you. That one card. Your mind and mine."

"At every moment in the history of magic, there is an anti-magician to go along with the mainstream magicians," Swiss says. The opposition between Vernon, the chamber genius, and Houdini, the charismatic star, goes on. The anti-magician of the moment is David Blaine, the patron saint of street and YouTube magic, the prophet of the new illusionism, but also its subverter.

Close up, Blaine is beautiful, in a 1950s, Actors Studio, young-Brando way, a perfect Jewish sheikh: hooded eyes, a high forehead, and a steady gaze, which he knows how to avert in awkward vulnerability. He wishes to press the edges of the form, and he believes that the future of magic lies in a naturalism beyond even Vernon's.

Blaine first became famous for doing tricks on television—some old and simple, some new and radical—but with the emphasis always on the faces of people, mostly girls, reacting with screams and gasps and semi-sexual eye rolling. ("Blaine saw something that we all saw, how people looked when they got 'fried,'" one old-timer says, "and then just turned the camera around.") Meanwhile, he never broke his air of moody, cool detachment.

He has a two-floor studio in Tribeca that is lined with magic posters of the great illusionists and seems usually to be accessorized with beautiful women, Nadias and Anyas. It tends also to be filled with a posse of purposeful young magicians in black, who both learn from Blaine and teach him—"He saved magic," one of them, the brilliant card man and street magician Daniel Garcia, said flatly—and is the center of a small, flourishing new enterprise, a kind of merger of magic with performance art. David Blaine has become best known for what he calls "endurance art," genuine, ungaffed daredevilry: standing on a pole for thirty-five hours, living in a water-filled plastic bubble or encased in ice. Not long ago, he claimed a record for the longest time spent underwater by a mammal, not counting a few species of whale.

"It's something I've been working my way around to," he murmured, talking about a project in which he planned to stay awake for a million seconds (11.57 days). "It started out just with lions." He shows an image he had photoshopped of himself as Daniel in Rubens's *Daniel in the Lions' Den*, a swarthy Brooklynite among the Baroque roarers. "But just being in a room with lions isn't about anything. So then I thought, What's the worst torture someone can undergo? And I realized it's going without sleep. So I researched it, you know, and found out what the record was. The guy who set the record didn't train for it, and he went kind of crazy afterward. I know I'll start to hallucinate and everything—but my idea is to do it outdoors and let people do anything they want to keep me awake. Stay awake for five days, and *then* bring out the lions." He makes his half smile.

"All my work is about honesty. Magic card tricks—we have to get beyond that. If magic is just magicians doing card tricks to impress other magicians—I'm not interested in that anymore. I don't want magic that looks real. What I want are real things that feel like magic."

His stunts are not stunts; they actually take place. His way of staying awake for a million seconds is to stay awake for a million seconds. There is a famous, and dangerous, illusionist's effect called the Bullet Catch; it is, of course, an elaborate and dangerous trick. Blaine insists that if he caught a bullet he would catch a bullet. "That's what Chris Burden did," he says, referring to the pioneering performance artist of the seventies, who did once have himself shot (in the arm) for art. "David Copperfield made the Statue of Liberty disappear, but then it came right back. My ideal magic would be *really* making the Statue of Liberty disappear, so that it never comes back, even if I have to go to jail afterward."

Las Vegas, at the MGM Grand: Swiss is about to go into David Copperfield's show while the banked drill of slot machines whir and ping nearby. It is sometime in the middle of the night, in a casino with no clocks or windows. Las Vegas is the last place in America where magic thrives in the normal American way: people get paid a lot to do it, and a lot of people pay to see it. Not as many as once did, perhaps—"I liked Vegas better when the Mob ran it" is the constant, semi-ironic complaint of the old-timers. They mean that the Mob's Vegas derived so much of its profit from gambling that the fun (and the food) could be given away more or less free, and a lounge could sponsor a closeup magician just because the owner liked him. These days, many show rooms are "four-walled," leased out by the owner and expected to be profit centers in themselves. Nonetheless, Big Magic, at least—the modern version of the splashy disappearing-girl shows that were once magic's mainstay—continues to flourish. Performers such as Lance Burton, Penn & Teller, and David Copperfield have successful shows that have run for years.

Swiss is talking about the recent past of Big Illusion: "After *The Ed Sullivan Show* ended, and before Doug Henning, there was nothing. There was always some guy out there somewhere sawing a woman, but that was it. Doug Henning did what Robert-Houdin set out to do—he presented magic in the dress of the time, only now it was tie-dye and long hair and hippieness. That saved illusion, at least on television. And then Copperfield came along. Copperfield—I remember when he was still calling himself Davino, at Tannen's." He shakes his head.

A stranger comes by and greets Swiss, a little warily. They exchange some magic shoptalk. Swiss laughs as the man walks off. "I got into a *bitter* argument with that guy at the Magic Castle last month. He was telling a young magician about the necessity of being pragmatic, making compromises for your art, and I said, 'What the fuck do you know about a work of art, or what it takes to make one!'" He smiles sheepishly. Like many combative souls, he takes his feuds and eruptions as part of the weather in his world, and assumes that his disputants do too.

Copperfield's show turns out to be much more loose-limbed and intelligent than his reputation for big dumb-stunt illusions suggests. He does the expected things—levitates through a steel plate, and makes thirteen audience members disappear (and reappear, at the back of the auditorium, where they giggle slightly in ways suggesting that their disappearance was less confounding than it seemed). But his oddly touching pièce de résistance is a confessional number about his father's failed career as an actor, and his own estrangement from his grandfather, and the old man's dream of one day winning the lottery and buying a green Lincoln Continental—probably the only case of a sad-bad-parenting memoir that ends with the thumping appearance on a Las Vegas stage of an actual green Lincoln.

After the show, over omelets at the Peppermill, a Las Vegas institution and show-biz hangout at the older, northern end of the Strip, Swiss meditates on the difference between the way audiences experience an illusion show now and the way they did a century ago. "It's a good show, a fun show—who can deny it? But what do people come to a Big Magic show for now? Celebrity? To be amazed? What did they come for then? Of course, there was less to see in the world then. They weren't going home to watch television. But I think they were there for beauty too. A lot of what magicians did then was just meant to be beautiful. It got that *Ahhh* sound you hear when Teller does the goldfish." He meant a signature Penn & Teller piece in which Teller turns water into silver coins and the coins into goldfish. "David Ben does an illusion show set in 1909, and, because it's set then, he does it much slower than we do now. And that kind of stage slowness turns out to be the right speed for magic. It isn't a high-speed art. The beauty lies in the unfolding, not in being zapped to the finish. It does for me, anyway. Onstage, it takes me three minutes to say my name."

The next night, David Copperfield takes Jamy Ian Swiss and the twelve-year-old and a mysterious family of Russians to his warehouse of magical paraphernalia. As they ride there in a limo, Copperfield explains the origins of his collection—it is a much larger version of the famous Mulholland collection—and hints at its treasures, largely, it seems, for Swiss's benefit. In photographs, Copperfield assumes a manner of chilly mastery; in person he is open, bending, almost needy, reminding the world of his triumphs—his renown, his Emmys—as though the scale of his accomplishments still surprised him too.

"Jamy? You'll be amazed when you see what I have at the warehouse," Copperfield says. "You were at Tannen's, too, right? Of course you were! I loved it with Lou. Did you know Lou? Did you see me in the Jubilee the year I was eighteen, when they gave me the whole second half?"

The warehouse is the size of an airplane hangar, windowless and fluorescent-lit in the Vegas night. Copperfield has been building it for years and has no intention of making it public; he offers tours, guided by him, as he thinks they are merited. Upstairs, he shows Swiss one beautiful piece after another, in spotlit cases. Everything is here. There are boxes of off-the-shelf magic sets for boys—a century's worth, stacked high into the air. There are the great monochrome posters of Alexander, the Man Who Knows; and posters of Charles Carter, in Egypt, being hanged, fighting the Devil himself. There is the complete outfit and wiring of the performer Mr. Electric, an *Ed Sullivan* regular. And there is nearly everything of Houdini's that matters: the original milk can that Houdini escaped from; one of the Metamorphosis Trunks (a fragment of the True Cross); and, on wax cylinders, the only recordings of Houdini's voice, high and hectoring and European-sounding as he does his patter.

There is the gun with which the great Chung Ling Soo (actually an American named William Ellsworth Robinson) was killed onstage at the Wood Green Empire, in London, in 1918, when his Bullet Catch number hit a snag. ("Oh my God. Something's happened. Lower the curtain" were his last words onstage, and the first ones he had spoken there in English for almost twenty years.) The apparatus for a Carter number, where a girl was pulled up in a chair, and then disappeared, shows the way the little chair gets hoisted into the framework of the machinery, leaving the damsel suspended. There is the sawing table where Orson Welles sawed Marlene Dietrich in half. Then, there are the automatons that Robert-Houdin built in the mid-nineteenth century, tiny clicking cogs and wheels and whirring clockwork: a brass Chinaman actually does the cups and balls, and each time the cups come up something new is underneath them. And books, wall after wall of bookshelves, with not only Max Malini's original copy of Erdnase but also a first edition of *Discoverie of Witchcraft* and the writings of Méliès, the French magician who invented special effects (dissolves, double exposures) in early movies—the effects that doomed Big Magic.

And then there is a wall of old signed publicity photographs of magicians: magicians with top hats, magicians resting their hands sapiently on their bearded cheeks; magicians grave and sage and, sometimes, witty and waggish, in top hats and tails, rising from floor to ceiling.

"Jamy? Do you see what it is?" David Copperfield says, triumphant.

"It's the wall from Tannen's," Swiss says softly, looking up at it as he must have done as a twelve-year-old. "It's the original photographs they had up, intact," he tells the twelve-year-old with him. The magicians, shining and unchanged since the '60s, beam down on their protégés, as though Lou were still behind the counter below.

Finally, in a small, crowded space upstairs, Copperfield carefully displays a legendary apparatus: the flower vase of Karl Germain, the great Cleveland-born magician. The vase stands up, music plays, a pass is made—and a whole rosebush slowly rises from inside, higher and higher, the petals of the roses unfolding as though waking up. The music plays, the roses grow and grow, higher and higher still, petals unfolding, and Copperfield cuts them off and gives one to each woman in the room.

How does it work? Where do the roses come from? One difficulty in writing about magic is that it is considered a cardinal sin to reveal methods, even when you are an outsider who barely grasps them—particularly when you are an outsider who barely grasps them. "Exposure" is a hanging crime in the magic world. In the '80s, Penn and Teller provoked hack magicians to attack them for doing the cups and balls in transparent glasses. (Of course, they did it so nimbly and surprisingly that they exposed nothing but the absurdity of "exposure.") About all an outsider may say is that the surprising thing about most magical methods is not how ingeniously complex they are but how extremely *stupid* they are—stupid, that is, in the sense of being completely obvious once you grasp them.

The trick to Swiss's Color Vision box, to engage in an exposure that is surely harmless, since his cousin Sharon knows all about it (and has had forty years to tell her friends, indignantly), is that the lid of the box is secretly moved by the magician to the side of the box; that is, the magician has revolved the box so that the top is now the back, and the lid is on what is now the side. He sees what the color is just by looking at it. What this teaches us is not that people are stupid but that the concept of rotating an object, though obvious, is in some way defeated by our familiarity with boxes and lids—a lid always goes on top. The move is not outside our imaginations but remote from our experience.

Most big illusions, similarly, involve a remarkably limited, though resourcefully manipulated, arsenal of mirrors and lights. We will ourselves both to overlook the obvious chicanery and to overrate the apparent obstacles. Or we imagine that an elaborate bit of trickery couldn't be achieved by stupidly obvious means, just as the Turk was among the first to demonstrate that people participate in their own illusions. That is why a magician's technique must be invisible; if it became visible, we would be insulted by its obviousness. Magic is possible because magicians are smart. And what they're smart about is mainly how dumb we are, how limited in vision, how narrow in imagination, how resourceless in conjecture, how routinized in our theories of the world, how deadened to possibility. The magician awakens us from the dogmatic slumbers of our daily life, our interactions with cards and hoops and things. He opens a door by pointing to a window.

Why does it matter? "Magic is the most intrinsically ironic of all the arts," Teller is saying. "I don't know what your definition of irony is, but mine is something where, when you are seeing it, you see it in two different and even contradictory ways at the same time. And with magic what you see collides with what you know. That's why magic, even when merely executed, ends up having intellectual content. It's intrinsic to the form."

Onstage, Teller's character is mute. In his own house—twenty minutes outside Las Vegas, an Expressionist concrete box, a stone fortress with trapezoidal windows cut in it, Dr. Caligari's remake of the Whitney Museum—over excellent cornmeal waffles, he is voluble, articulate, opinionated, and exact. Small and curly-haired, he looks like Harpo Marx released from his vow of silence and given tenure.

His is one of those houses perfectly shaped to the needs of their fastidious and eccentric owners: it is hung with his father's paintings; there is a beautiful coffin, given to him by a close friend for his fifty-fifth birthday, and a handsome dining table with a skeleton embedded in its glass top, its arms and feet shackled to a rack. (To extend the table for company, you turn a crank, which stretches out the skeleton, causing moans and screams to sound through a concealed speaker.) Bookcases revolve and reveal secret passageways to the next room. Though it is April, the Christmas tree is still up, and decorated with skulls and metallic-red devils' heads.

"There is a more romantic way to do it, to calm down the intrinsic irony, but that can get schmaltzy," he goes on. "Many magicians do that, but it tends toward the sentimental."

In Las Vegas, Penn & Teller have not compromised their act. They do a flag burning onstage—or, rather, seem to do it—before restoring the flag completely, in a variation of the torn-and-restored dollar; it's a heartfelt libertarian tribute to American freedom. And they end with a staggering Bullet Catch, the stunt that killed Chung Ling Soo. (Someone remarks to Teller that the Bullet Catch seems to be the *Macbeth* of magic, the bad-luck piece, and he says, dryly, "Yes. You're standing onstage firing bullets at the magician with a live gun. That might be bad luck.")

Swiss tells Teller about the tour of the Copperfield warehouse and his rediscovery of the wall from Tannen's. Though Teller grew up in Philadelphia, he recognizes the key moment memorialized by the wall. "There's a moment in your life when you realize the difference between illusion and reality and that you're being lied to," he says. "Santa Claus. The Easter Bunny. After my mother told me that there was no Santa Claus, I made up an entirely fictitious girl in my classroom and told my mother stories about *her*. Then I told my mother, 'You know what—she isn't real.'" He smiles with somewhat Pugsley Addams–like glee, and goes on, more soberly, "If you're sufficiently preoccupied with the power of a lie, a falsehood, an illusion, you remain interested in magic tricks."

The subject of the Germain vase comes up, and Teller says, "You know the funny thing about that? A friend and I did the

Germain flowers last year. We put the music on, the *right* music played at the right time, slightly off speed, and we prepped the illusion properly, you know, had the buds set right so that they would open when you fanned them—the fanning is part of the piece—and we watched it emerge. This lovely music was playing, and we just *wept* at the beauty of it—tears streamed down our cheeks at the lovely apparition of it. That was magic."

Of all the arguments that can preoccupy the mindful magician, the most important involves what is called the Too Perfect theory. Jamy Ian Swiss has written about it often. Presaged by Vernon himself, and formalized by the illusionist Rick Johnsson in a 1971 article, the Too Perfect theory says, basically, that any trick that simply astounds will give itself away. If, for instance, a magician smokes a cigarette and then makes it pass through an ordinary quarter, the only reasonable explanation is that it isn't an ordinary quarter; the spectator will immediately know that it's a trick quarter, with a hinge. (Swiss wrote that once, after he performed the Cigarette Through Quarter—perfectly, in his opinion—a spectator responded, "Neat. Where's that nifty coin with the hole in it?")

What makes a trick work is not the inherent astoundingness of its effect but the magician's ability to suggest any number of possible explanations, none of them conclusive, and none of them quite obvious. As the law professor and magician Christopher Hanna has noted, two of the best ways of making a too-perfect trick work are "reducing the claim" and "raising the proof." Reducing the claim means roughing up the illusion so that the spectator isn't even sure she saw one—bringing the cigarette in and out of the coin so quickly that the viewer doesn't know if the trick is in the coin or in her eyes. Raising the proof is more demanding. Derek Dingle, a famous closeup man, adjusted the

Cigarette Through Quarter trick by palming and replacing one gaffed quarter with another. One quarter had a small hole in it, the other a spring hinge. By exposing the holed coin, then palming that one and replacing it with the hinged coin, he led the spectator to think not *There must be two trick coins* but *How could even the trick coin I've seen do* that *trick?* Or one might multiply the possible explanations, in a card-guessing trick, by going through an elaborate charade of "reading" the spectator's face and voice, so that, when the forced card is guessed, the obviousness of the trick is, well, obviated.

At the heart of the Too Perfect theory is the insight that magic works best when the illusions it creates are open-ended enough to invite the viewer into a credibly imperfect world. Magic is the dramatization of explanation more than it is the engineering of effects. In every art, the Too Perfect theory helps explain why people are more convinced by an imperfect, "distressed" illusion than by a perfectly realized one. A form of the theory is involved when special-effects people talk about "selling the shot" in a movie; that is, making sure that the speeding spacecraft or the raging Godzilla doesn't look too neatly and cosmetically packaged, and that it is not lingered on long enough to be really seen. (All special effects appear as such when they are studied.) The theory explains the force of the off-slant scene in a film, the power of elliptical dialogue in the theatre, the constant artistic need to turn away from apparent perfection toward the laconic or unfixed. Illusion affects us only when it is incomplete.

But the Too Perfect theory has larger meanings too. It reminds us that, whatever the context, the empathetic interchange between minds is satisfying only when it is "dynamic," unfinished, unresolved. Friendships, flirtations, even love affairs depend, like magic tricks, on a constant exchange of incomplete but tantalizing information. We are always reducing the claim or raising the proof. The master magician teaches us that romance lies in an unstable contest of minds that leaves us knowing it's a trick but not which one it is, and being impressed by the other person's ability to let the trickery go on. Frauds master our minds; magicians, like poets and lovers, engage them in a permanent maze of possibilities. The trick is to renew the possibilities, to keep them from becoming schematized, to let them be imperfect, and the question between us is always "Who's the magician?" When we say that love is magic, we are telling a truth deeper, and more ambiguous, than we know.

Swiss is talking over dinner about the Too Perfect theory: "What magic is out to do isn't just to amaze you but to achieve what Whit Haydn calls putting 'a burr under the saddle of the mind.'" He leaps up from the table and becomes a man on a tightrope. "Let's say you do a Blaine trick, one he's done on television, where you have someone choose a card and then find it in a sealed basketball. Well, if he sees it in the basketball he knows that somehow the card's been forced on him. It's too perfect. But if it's got a torn corner—or it's signed, or if maybe instead of being inside a basketball it's behind a backboard—he thinks, It wasn't there before, but he can't get over there. The mind starts working. He can't rest here, he can't rest here, and he stays on the tightrope!" Swiss wavers on the imaginary wire.

"That's not the situation of the passive dupe," he says, sitting down. "It's the situation of someone whose mind is alive! It's the state of the scientist, or the artist—and magic is a fringe art, but it's not a fringe subject. Truth, deception, and mystery are big material, and they're the natural, the intrinsic subject of magic. And I propose"—he smiles briefly at the formulation but goes ahead anyway—"that it's the only art form where that's the intrinsic subject. And that's why, with all the indignities and absurdities of being a professional magician, we'll always need magic."

David Blaine was on a strict new regimen as he trained for the sleepless piece. Once a week, he ran thirteen miles in Central Park, played basketball for an hour and a half at Chelsea Piers, and then swam several miles in a downtown pool. It was his theory that a man in perfect form will be able to survive staying awake for a million seconds. By the time I spoke with him, he had already lost forty pounds, and this gave him a gaunt, spiritualized look, like the young Brando playing an AIDS patient. He was in his Greenwich Village apartment, showing a protégé a card trick and quizzing him, gently, on a book about the Holocaust that he had given him to read. The first vibe you get from him, of cool and insolence, is soon succeeded by a second, truer sense that he is a man trying to save magic not by making it more intellectual, or more raffish, but by making it potentially tragic, a high-stakes and risky endeavor that might end in grief.

———

BLAINE STILL WORKS intently on card tricks, of the more avant-garde kind that derive from the great Spanish magician Juan Tamariz, whom all magicians today, on all sides, uncritically revere. The card trick he is teaching his protégé involves no apparent skill, no card handling or card moving, still mind against mind, but without the interference of fingers. The effect is powerful, but the vibe is different from normal card tricks: melodramatic rather than clever, and deep rather than ironic. The odd thing is that, the longer one knows him, and the more time one spends with him, the more apparent it becomes that he is one more Tannen's boy from Brooklyn. On his desk is a photograph of the adolescent Blaine collecting an award at Tannen's summer camp, as nerdy and needy as every other boy of the tribe.

"My real work began when I was walking down the street, just practicing a one-handed shuffle, and all the guys in this garage I was walking by went *Ohhhh!*" Blaine says. "*Ohhhh!*—just for a shuffle! I started realizing that what I love to do is bring magic for one second—and that one second is enough. My endurance pieces are all about taking away the ego, putting yourself in a position so intense that the ordinary 'I' doesn't exist anymore. You're surviving the way a baby does—or it's like just before an accident, when you see everything, the seats and the road, and the dashboard and your life, in slow motion. That heightened sense of awareness, the blinding flash of being shocked out of your logical mind—that's magic for me."

For Jamy Ian Swiss, as for Penn & Teller, the future lies in magic being remade in the light of the real but still in the shadow of the past, losing the false front while revering the traditional techniques. For David Blaine, it lies in an increasing encroachment into the real, so that magic will become indistinguishable from performance art, at the high end, and reality television, at the low. The choice, in a sense, is between the real work and the real thing.

I have seen Blaine and Swiss together just once. It was a few months before the annual auction of magic posters and paraphernalia at Swann Galleries, on East Twenty-Fifth Street, an important occasion in the magic subculture. Swiss was once quoted as saying that Blaine's best tricks could have been purchased for thirty dollars at a Times Square magic shop, a quote that was taken slightly out of context, and that had a gentler intention than it seems. Now, with the tough critic's optimistic belief that it was all part of the game, Swiss went up to Blaine and congratulated him. Then Swiss mentioned a young student of his who had been hanging around with Blaine as well.

"I'm trying to get him to see some of the—some of the deeper psychological things, not just tricks," Blaine said, in his Brando mumble.

"I don't think I'm showing him tricks," Swiss said.

"Not tricks, man. I mean—you know, techniques. Showing him something deeper than techniques."

"I'm not showing him tricks," Swiss repeated quietly.

Blaine changed the subject.

Swiss went back to his seat, with his head down, his jaw set. I could see him struggling with the times—with the anger of feeling a protégé being fought over but also with the sense, which every writer knows, of helplessness in the face of the new thing, of suddenly knowing what the real fringe is like, and how it feels when you get there. We are all magicians now. The same feeling that novelists had when first confronted with movies is shared by closeup-card magicians confronting television endurance artists—the feeling that something big and vital is passing from the world, and yet that to defend it is to be immediately classified as retrograde.

I saw, too, that David Blaine is absolutely sincere in his belief that the way forward for a young magician lies not in mastering the tricks but in mastering the mind of the modern age, with its relentless appetite for speed and for the sensational-dressed-as-the-real. And I thought I sensed in Swiss the urge to say what all of us would like to say—that traditions are not just encumbrances, that a novel is not news, that an essay is a different thing from an Internet rant, that techniques are the probity and ethic of magic, the real work. The crafts that we have mastered are, in part, the tricks that we have learned, and though we know how much knowledge the tricks enfold, still, tricks is what they are. I felt for Jamy, and for us, and for the boy caught between.

The hands stop moving as the plane lands, and the boy and the magician leave. The aces twist one turn and the boy returns to his father for the car ride home. He clutches his Las Vegas souvenir. The magicians have the boys for a moment, between their escape from their fathers and their pursuit of girls. After that, they become sexual, outwardly so, and learn that women (or other men) cannot be impressed by tricks of any kind: if they are watching at all, they are as interested as they are ever going to be, and tricks are of no help. You cannot woo anyone with magic; the magic that you have consciously mastered is the least interesting magic you have.

Yet, for the time being, what the magicians teach the boys is that some knowledge cannot be communicated; it is yours and can only be shown, and the range of things that fathers don't know is larger than what they do. The most the father can hope to become is a stooge, a willing assistant, and a spectator with a bit of corruption. The boy has secret knowledge, which he will keep, even after life arrives and magic stops.

Teach me a trick, the father says to the son, and the boy (for it is his son, his alone, coming back now to his normal place in the family deck, like a briefly vanished ace) with his hands working the cards, says, "I can't teach you a trick, Dad. I'll show you an effect." And then he does, doing passes, like his teacher, all the way home. The card always comes back to the top of the deck, and, the better it is done, the harder it is to see that anything has happened at all.

The Second Mystery
of Mastery

Erdnase, or, The Mystery of Identity
and Intention

M Y TIME AMONG THE MAGICIANS MADE ME
aware, again and again, of one of the greatest mysteries
in magic: not how the lower half of the woman keeps wriggling
its toes while the upper half keeps talking, nor how David Copperfield makes the Statue of Liberty disappear, but the simple
question, still unanswered after a century of asking: Who was
S. W. Erdnase?

Erdnase is everywhere. When Jamy Ian Swiss cried out, in
David Copperfield's warehouse, "It's Malini's Erdnase!" the reason for his excitement seemed self-evident to the other magicians,
old and young. He is the subtext, and sometimes the ur-text,
of so much else. Erdnase is the author named on the title page
of the early-twentieth-century volume *The Expert at the Card
Table*, also called *Artifice Ruse and Subterfuge at the Card Table:
A Treatise on the Science and Art of Manipulating Cards*, which is
the holy volume of modern magic. (The first title is on the book's
cover; the second on its title page.) I write "modern magic"
rather than only modern *card* magic, because the philosophy it
entails, one of extreme "naturalism" in all things performative,
has a much broader application. Even Penn & Teller's offhand

charm descends from Erdnase's insistence in making every move in magic look like anything except a move in magic. "Within the pages," magician Lance Pierce has written, "is embodied an entire philosophy of conduct and manner, a cogent and complete system of thinking about magic and its related fields. Far beyond the wonderful moves contained therein, what the book gives us is an approach, a style, and a guidebook toward really understanding not only the inner workings and mechanisms of sleight of hand, but its psychology and practice as well—and because of this, much of what it has to say goes way beyond the field of card work alone. Sometimes it seems almost as though everything every great magician has said about performance and execution is already there in the pages of this book, concisely stated and well-phrased."

Published by the author himself in 1902, in Chicago, deftly and profusely illustrated by one M. D. Smith—the illustrations are line drawings of hands, frozen in the midst of intricate action—the book offers a promise from its author on its opening page: Erdnase will teach anyone who reads it the mastery of card manipulation, and also that he will "use no sophistry as an excuse for its existence. The hypocritical cant of reformed gamblers(?), or whining mealy mo[u]thed pretensions of piety are not foisted as a justification for imparting the knowledge it contains . . . it will not make the innocent vicious, or transform the pastime player into a professional; or make the fool wise, or curtail the annual crop of suckers; but whatever the result may be, if it sells it will accomplish the primary motive of the author, as he needs the money."

"Erdnase" is referencing, with his ironic interrogation mark, the many contemporary books that claimed to be written by gamblers-gone-good and that disclosed secrets in order to warn off the unwary, *Music Man*–style, from games of chance gone bad. (With the implication that, exactly in *Music Man* style, the real motive of their authors was making money, not doing good.) But the entire passage suggests some of the book's resonant charm. Erdnase is, even by late-nineteenth-century standards, an ornate and orotund writer who has fully mastered the then-vanishing Johnsonian sentence, with its careful, Latinate balancings—"It may caution the unwary who are innocent of guile, and it may inspire the craft by enlightenment on artifice," he writes elsewhere, "it" being his book—adding to it a nice feeling for the Mark Twain–style, flat American drop-in clause. (For example, "as he needs the money.") Erdnase, cagily, never says directly that he made his living cheating at cards—perhaps for obvious reasons, perhaps for reasons more obscure—but that is certainly the strong implication any reader of the book, then or now, would take away from it.

The bulk of "The Expert" is taken up by maniacally detailed instructions, a model for technical writing of all kinds, for card handling, as in his exquisitely precise description of the stock shuffle, in which a set of cards is sneakily drawn from the bottom of the deck in the midst of an innocent-seeming mix before dealing:

Run several cards into the left hand, but well down into the palm, so that the second and third fingers protrude to the first joints from underneath—then, when the right hand has made the next downward motion, instead of drawing off the top card with the left thumb, press the left second and third fingertips against the bottom card and let it slide into the left hand, drawn into position on the other cards with the left thumb as the right hand is raised. (See Fig. 32.)

Fig. 32, seen and examined, enlarges but hardly clarifies the intricacy of the move. But for magicians, Erdnase is equally legendary for his firm injunctions and slightly enigmatic aphorisms: "To be suspected of a skill is a death blow to the professional"; "Excessive vanity proves the undoing of many experts"; and, perhaps the most celebrated observation, "The resourceful professional failing to improve the method changes the moment." (Some commas would help the sense there. He means, make the spectator, or the marks, pay attention to the *wrong* moment, while you do the method—that is, the move, before or after.) Bottom dealing, passes, and palming—the basic repertoire of card magic—if it scarcely begins with Erdnase, got its first encyclopedic characterization here.

Most foundational books inevitably stand on some other foundation—how can they not? Perspective drawing has many improvisational origins in Italian art before it is codified by the architects Alberti and Brunelleschi—and the musicologists assure us that Bach's well-tempered clavier had been, perhaps somewhat less well tempered, but still well-enough tempered to count, well before Bach. We pygmies stand on the shoulders of giants, as Newton's famous aphorism has it, but even giants stand on the shoulders of other, older giants. Long lists of earlier books that contained the same card moves Erdnase presented can be composed. Some of those books are much earlier, some, suspiciously, only a few years earlier, and some, curiously, or perhaps significantly, had been published only in German. In 1991, magician Darwin Ortiz, in one of the more remarkable works of scholarship in a specialized field, published his *Annotated Erdnase*, which tracks many of the moves to their earlier sources and provides a Talmudic commentary on the book as long as the original.

Books are so honored only when they matter. Yet, as with most breakthrough systems, its honored place was won by a single practitioner. It was because a young Canadian boy living in Ottawa was given a copy of *The Expert* by his father, who worked for the government copyright office, that it became the "Bible" of manipulation. Dai Vernon, that boy, spent his boyhood immersed in Erdnase, and his lifelong evangelism for the primacy of the book was what made Erdnase the essential guide to card magic for many generations—to the point, as I've said, that young magicians may keep an octavo, fine-print copy in their inside pocket as a talisman and tutor both.

The book is, appropriately for a Bible, divided in half, with a kind of Old and New Testament double-shuffle. The first part of the book is devoted to moves a card cheat, the expert at the card table, would need to master; the second part to "legerdemain"—magic tricks exhibited as such, with elaborate and sonorous "patter" supplied. (The late card shark and magic-curator and performer Ricky Jay would perform one of these tricks in his act, more for the sound of the talk than for the glory of the gaff.) It has been argued that the "legerdemain" section was put in, reluctantly, to help the book sell, with assistance likely from one James Harto, "a magician who ran a magic shop in Indianapolis."

Okay. But who *was* he? The name S. W. Erdnase is an obvious pseudonym, occurring in no other public record; as early as the 1920s, through inquiries made with the publisher of the second edition, it became known that S. W. Erdnase was most probably an anagram, flipped around, for the name E. S. Andrews. And so, among Erdnase obsessives, the search for a card shark or player named E. S. Andrews, or something very close to that, who might have had a reason to make public his methods in 1902 and then, somehow, entirely mysteriously disappeared after, became a subsidiary B-plot in the history of magic.

No one was more dogged in the search than that great American maverick intellectual Martin Gardner. Gardner, the author of *The Annotated Alice* and *Annotated Snark*, which invented the still-living genre of the richly and speculatively footnoted classic, of which Ortiz's tome is a later instance, was, among other countless interests, an amateur magician. When still a young man, in the 1940s, he thought that he had stumbled on the key to the Erdnase mysteries. Searching in Chicago for information on Erdnase, he found in the phone book, somewhat to his shock, the very M. D. Smith who had illustrated the book—and who, far from having disappeared himself into the mists of artisanal work, was still alive and working and glad to speak. Smith did have a few memories of Erdnase, though they were of the tantalizingly fragmentary kind that would be natural in remembering something that had happened almost a half century ago and that, at the time, seemed to be of little consequence. His name was, yes, Andrews; Smith had met him in a drafty Chicago hotel room; he was dapper and seemed well educated and well spoken; he was short; he was proud of his soft hands; at some point he mentioned in passing a family connection to the cartoonist Lewis Dalrymple.

With that, and with more information supplied by an "old-time gambler living in Philadelphia" named Edgar Lawton Pratt, who claimed to have known Erdnase (whom he called "Andrews" throughout their correspondence), Gardner landed on a candidate for authorship: one Milton Andrews, a card cheat who had died by vivid, not to say melodramatic, means, shooting himself, along with a young woman he was having an affair with, as the police came to arrest him in a murder case. "The end of Andrews is not pleasant to read, write or think about," Pratt had assured Gardner, and this story certainly seemed to fit.

Expert opinion has long moved on from Milton Andrews, treating him as an impossible candidate—wrong shape, wrong age, wrong spirit—despite the firm word of Pratt, who alone among the informants could confidently claim firsthand knowledge of the original. (Or was a career card cheat amusing himself with one last scam?) And so, the search for Erdnase—which became, in effect, the search for the right Andrews—continued, and continues, in online magic forums and in specialized publications, to this day. The candidates are introduced hopefully and breathlessly, rather like the candidates who supposedly "really" wrote Shakespeare, with the significant difference that no one but Shakespeare wrote Shakespeare, and in this case, someone not named S. W. Erdnase really did write the book assigned to him.

Over the years, pretty much anyone named Andrews who can be shown to have held a deck of cards in the 1890s, or anyone who can be shown to have held a deck of cards in the 1890s and whose name can somehow be twisted into something like Andrews, gets an audition. There is a writer named James J. Andrews (who published in *Harper's*, in 1909, an article called "The Confessions of a Fakir"); a casino owner and expert card dealer named James M. Andrews; a riverboat captain named E. S. Andrews; an engineer named E. S. Andrews; and a newspaper publisher named, of course, E. S. Andrews. Edwin Summer Andrews was a railroad agent at a time when trains were the place that cards got played, who was married to a woman named Seely with a potential connection to Dalrymple. He's a candidate. An even better one is a W. E. Sanders: Wilbur Edgerton Sanders, a mining engineer, with links to card playing.

Each candidate, as in other mysteries of the type, has some intriguing overlap with what's known about Erdnase, and, invariably, some incongruence that would seem disqualifying. Wilbur Egerton Sanders for instance, was well educated and had gone to Columbia and had in his published writing an orotund style not unlike Erdnase's, as well as a reason for his concealment: his father was a U.S. senator. (And that father was once, it seems, caricatured by the cartoonist Dalrymple!) Even the name "Erdnase" is a German pun for "earth nose," not a bad description of a mining engineer.

Yet the image we have from Smith of the real Erdnase, shivering in a Chicago hotel room, showing off his soft hands, working through a hundred illustrations on a card table, hardly matches that of a successful engineer who played cards on the side. It doesn't seem plausible that the degree of care and the obvious note-by-note absorption of the work in *Expert* would be compatible with a full-time career in another, equally demanding field. He may have relied on imposture and deliberate subterfuge, but Erdnase certainly doesn't *sound* like a senator's son making a good living in a prestigious field who spends his holiday time cheating at cards. He *sounds* like someone who spent most of his time cheating at cards. The consensus was that somewhere, perhaps among one of these men, was a card shark, or even a cheat who, for family reasons or for reasons of personal or professional "prestige," didn't want anyone to know what he did and preferred to hide behind a pseudonym while still sharing his clearly obsessional relationship to card technique. To locate Erdnase one had to locate him within the glamorous, shadow world of turn-of-the century gambling; you'd be looking for a man familiar with smoking-car poker games and posh but secret gambling establishments off small Chicago streets. An enigma of intention wrapped within a riddle of identity, Erdnase hovered as a dark figure from an early, silent noir movie, or as an invisible Keyser Söze of cards.

————

AND THAT WAS where the mystery stood until, in 2020, the greatest card manipulator of our own time, Steve Forte, published his "case against Erdnase." In a privately printed book with the punning title *Gambling Sleight of Hand: Forte Years of Research*, much of it turning on technical questions of card handling that only another card handler could judge, Forte argues that both Erdnase's book, and his credentials, are vastly overrated, to the point of deliberate fraud. We were barking up the wrong tree because we were looking for the wrong guy. Erdnase wasn't a professional card cheat, or even an "expert at the card table." He was, most probably, a well-meaning amateur magician who had worked out a lot of gimmicks, some good, some shoddy, on his own, and was trying to pass himself off as the pro that he was not.

Forte was far from the first commentator to make the case that Erdnase was not in fact a professional card shark. But he had some curious credentials that made his case particularly credible. "The question of who the greatest card man is, is over. It's him," Jamy Ian Swiss, himself a candidate for the title, says flatly. ("There may be an argument about who's in fifth, sixth, or seventh place," he reports another magician as remarking, "But no argument about who's in first.") Forte's is a fascinating history. Having made himself into a genuine, up-to-date, master casino "advantage player," using both his extraordinary card skills and some high-tech systems, he ended up, after what seem to be some movie-worthy scores, in legal difficulty. He has also pursued a second career devoted to security work for vulnerable casinos;

how the two careers, as advantage player and casino protector, have entangled is a complex story, worth telling. (Needless to say, the Forte movie begins with an "in retirement" trope, where Matt Damon coaxes the greatest card man in the world back out for one last score.)

Much of what Forte has to say against Erdnase depends on technical details that a ham-handed amateur can neither judge nor often pretend to understand. But his indictment has an overall theme, one that has been offered before: cheating at cards is a far more improvisational, opportunistic, rough-edged, and dangerous activity than Erdnase's elegant performative moves suggest. Card cheats are iron-nerved mechanics who work one or two crude devices, usually in collusion with another cheater. Blue-collar plumbers of leaking human greed, the last thing in the world they want is an elegant shuffle, or a trick move, much less to be seen doing anything that even remotely resembles "work." When it comes to Erdnase's shifts—the delightful move, as we've seen, in which a simple cut of the cards actually conceals the interposition of a packet of chosen cards—Forte says: "Erdnase seems to base these moves on those employed by standup magicians and his one-handed shift is a perfect example of overkill in terms of pursuing the perfect move for all the wrong reasons." His grips would telegraph the work across the room; his bottom deals are transparent; he leaves out the more obvious and inelegant work, like marked cards and "cooler" decks, switched in rough edges, that are the actual real work of cheating and cheaters. "Erdnase's motive, thinking and lofty technical goals were often saddled with little or no monetary upside. This is not the way card cheaters think and operate." "In 20 minutes," he goes on, exasperated, "I can show you better, more practical, authentic gambling moves than Erdnase offered in *The Expert*."

Forte offers a neat reversal of what had long been the conventional view, which had Erdnase the master cheat sighing and adding a chapter on magic to help sell books. Far from having to have been persuaded by another party to include "legerdemain," Forte suggests, that was all he really knew, and the gambling moves, and the not-really-repentant card-shark history, represented his creation of a fantasy self. (Something that is oddly confirmed by an overlooked detail in M. D. Smith's memories, that Erdnase showed him a couple of card tricks before getting down to work, which is not something one would think would be the first practice of a professional cheat.)

The irony is perhaps more delicious than can quite be distilled from Forte's workmanlike prose. Erdnase was, in implicitly presenting himself as a cheater, cheating—and the form that his cheating took, in pretending to be a cheater, is typical of the way that cheaters cheat, even though in fact the kind of cheating he was doing was not the kind of cheating he claimed to have done. Not really a card cheat at all, he was the most impressive card *book* cheat writer there has ever been. And in that form of cheating, he used exactly the actual skills of a card cheat, which are not sophisticated moves and elegant devices but brazen nerve and cool imposition and a willingness to deceive, ruthlessly and relentlessly, taking on an assumed role with an almost frightening completeness. The con man and card cheat understand that we have a natural bent for taking other people at their own estimation, accepting their presented selves as identical with their actual selves. It is too painful and paranoid for us to do otherwise.

———

EVALUATING FORTE'S CRITICISM, the specific questions of magic technique and card handling are of course outside the competence of a non-magician, or even of anyone outside the very top range of card magic. And yet at the same time, in reading an expert on a single subject, one sees holes in their understanding of what *you* might be expert on. Once again, mastery turns out to be a many-sided thing, an atmospheric effect, and no one eye can analyze it all.

To take a simple instance, Forte speculates that Erdnase might have been writing as a syndicate, with collaborators, because he often uses the first-person plural—"We" used as if "I." Here, Forte makes a forgivable if egregious error. The first-person plural "we" was not only common in 1902, but it was also nearly universal in any explanatory or editorial writing of the time, and long after. E. B. White was still using that same "we" a quarter century later in his "Notes and Comment" in *The New Yorker*; indeed, it didn't disappear from the magazine until the 1990s. (I may have been the very last writer to employ it!) Any Chicago newspaper in 1902 would have used it. It was simply the way you wrote.

A subtler point lies in the matter of tone. Erdnase writes in the still formal, somewhat stilted, often delightfully mannered fashion of late-nineteenth-century popular prose. This is one reason why apparent resemblances between his style and that of the candidates for Erdnasehood are less significant than their devotees believe. When Sanders and Erdnase are both shown to use idioms like "a careful perusal of the following" or "may be employed advantageously," which sound highly specific to us now, when no one says "perusal," they are simply participating in a common rhetoric of the time. Erdnase, whoever he was, was a practitioner of the same omnipresent rhetorical style of 1902 that had ballplayers quoted in newspapers saying things like "Many of us on the ball club are frankly bewildered by the recent handling of the pitchers."

Yet those of us who have spent our lives reading and writing, handling words as magicians handle cards, come to know both the conscious and unconscious origins of a writer's voice—who he or she is and what they're hiding and what they can't hide. I recall reading, in Simon Singh's *Codebook*, about the so-called Beale ciphers mystery—nineteenth-century ciphers that pretend to point toward a buried treasure in Virginia—and sensed at once that they were an elaborate hoax, just by the tone and wording of the letters pretending to propound the mystery. They were trying too hard and reaching too obviously, specific where they might be general and generalized where they needed to be specific, and this I gather is now the consensus view of students of the cipher. I couldn't begin to break the cipher, but, having spent a lifetime reading, I could sense the sound of a fraud.

Strange as it may sound, as a writer I would bet money—not my life, perhaps, but money—that Erdnase was indeed an expert at the card table. That he had passed his life playing and manipulating cards, not as a Sunday hobbyist but as an obsessive, someone who for years had lived and slept with cards seems inescapably demonstrated by his sentences. Even Forte agrees that Erdnase is well written—but when we call a piece of nonfiction "well written" we don't mean that mean that its sentences capture the details of a subject in the fullness of their facticity. Erdnase isn't well written because of its vocabulary or some other kind of erudite eloquence. Erdnase is well written because each sentence has the tension and weight and communicative intensity of something genuinely experienced by the writer, like Hemingway on trout fishing. It may be that he didn't do it as a crook—and in truth he never quite says that he did—but that he did it for a living I have no doubt.

Deeper still in the mystery of identity and intention is a truth about reading *anything* from a time gone by. "The past is a foreign country; they do things differently there" is the opening line of L. P. Hartley's 1953 novel *The Go-Between,* and one can't write meaningfully about things past without keeping this in the forefront of your mind. Forte is judging the value and worth of Erdnase's sleights and potential for cheating by the standards of a Las Vegas casino (or a private card room in a modern hotel) in the year 2020, which has nothing to do with the practices and possibilities of a (gas-lit, shivering-cold) hotel room or parlor car on a railroad in 1902. We can't re-create their expectations, tastes, degrees of skilled observation, at least not without a herculean effort. They were credulous in ways we're not, just as they were sharp about things we no longer are. Bill James makes this point in one of his true-crime books—that a jury in 1920 who were easily bamboozled by bad fingerprint evidence were nonetheless sharp as tacks about a suspect piece of wood, since they had all worked with wood in ways we no longer are expected to—whereas we would be sharp about technical evidence, having trained on *Law & Order* and *CSI* for decades, and dumb as cattle about carpentry. Our expectations of what is and isn't natural at a card table have been changed, not least by the existence of Erdnase's book. Our sophistication in doing things is sharpened by our experiments in describing them. Each skilled description polishes the doing, which then points to imperfections in the description.

One suspects that if a skilled contemporary card man went into a card room to cheat in 1900, he'd be surprised by the relative ease with which you could fool players with some moves, and also surprised by what they noticed that you didn't think they would—by what they saw and didn't see. They'd be, perhaps, far more expert in card *playing* since they did it all the time, and far less conditioned to "look" for shifts and passes and the rest, since magic and its effects were less widely available.

I should add that Jamy Ian Swiss strongly disputes this idea, insisting that there are fixed continuities in card handling, and that "what works now would work then, and that perhaps what worked then in the hands of the expert would also work now." I think, though, that we all tend to accept the force of the "frame" in worlds not our own and underestimate them in those we know. A modern audio engineer might scoff at the idea that a wind-up Victrola hidden behind a curtain could be mistaken for an actual soprano—but this did indeed seem to happen at the beginning of recorded sound. Sommeliers are equally contemptuous of the idea that red and white wines are indistinguishable without visual clues—but here again this seems at least in some conditions to be the case. I know that I would scoff at the notion that I could ever be fooled by a fake Picasso or a phony Shakespeare sonnet—but better scholars than I are fooled all the time. And no "frame" is more powerful than the past. The conditions of card cheating are obviously in some ways constant and in some ways—think of the lighting of rooms, the style and heft of the clothes worn, or just the prevalence of cigar and cigarette smoke—very different, and what weighs and what doesn't on any effect is hard to know in the abstract. In the simple but wise words of our parents: You really had to be there. And we're not. (Once, on the track of the words spoken at Lincoln's deathbed by Edwin Stanton, I entertained countless subtle arguments—and then discovered, visiting it, that the room in which he died was so astoundingly small and crowded that any words would have been drowned out by the ambient noise of the people forcing their way inside.)

Which is not to say that the past is unobtainable. Only that it is remote and needs to be treated with the respect we give to remote locations on the planet now, recognizing a fragile ecology not our own.

———

WELL, REALLY, what does it matter what Erdnase's identity really was, or what his intention might have been? The book—the work, the "room"—is there. But this ignores the larger point. Identity and intention are essential to our experience of performance of any kind, mastery in all its guises, art in all its forms, high and low and in-between.

The case of the contemporary translations, or rather non-translations, of the Persian poets Rumi and Hafez might help us see why who made it matters to what we think "it" is. Both Rumi and Hafez were medieval Persian poets, mystics with enormous reputations in their native culture. Both became deeply beloved in the past thirty or forty years in English and American translation, becoming among the most cited and beloved of all meme-makers. Beautiful phrases, expressing a kind of everyday mysticism, of love found in small things, flowed from them into pop-song lyrics and illustrated calendars: "If you are irritated by every rub, / how will your mirror be polished?" or, "Every moment I shape my destiny with a chisel. I am a carpenter of my own soul." Leonard Cohen was a particularly intense fan of Rumi, borrowing in song his thought that it is the crevices within our lives that offer the most chance for illumination to leak through.

Yet Persian speakers and students of Muslim mysticism warn us that, in truth, the Rumi and Hafez we are responding to with such joy are almost entirely modern American inventions, "translated" by American poets with little knowledge of the original language. In one case, a "translator" openly admits that he has a kind of mystical charge to "translate" Hafez by a kind of spirit-writing, letting the Persian poet's spirit invade his own. Many of the poems published under Hafez's name are this modern poet's own inventions. Even when there is an underlying source, the poets have been stripped, for good or ill, of their Muslim piety, and of their actual period feeling. One famous Rumi verse, for instance, reads literally, "If any man asks you about the houris, show your face, saying, 'Like this.'" But "houris" are the virgins promised in Paradise to pious Muslims, and therefore more than a little outside the range of contemporary American sensibilities. And so the line, in its most familiar translation, becomes, "If anyone asks you / how the perfect satisfaction / of all our sexual wanting / will look, lift your face / and say, / Like this." It isn't just that it's fake exoticism, which can be very beautiful. Whistler's Japonisme, or Edward FitzGerald's translation of the Rubaiyat of Omar Khayyam, are both equally "spurious" representations of a foreign sensibility. But we recognize the filter of the past through which they've passed and for the most part their time recognized that filter too. They may be the real work, but we know they're not the real thing.

What we love, or loved, in those Rumi and Hafez poems are the sense that they are just that—not just the real work but the real thing. They provide us with a feeling, against all odds, of being *close*, of sharing, despite the vast gap in time and faith that separates us, in a common sensibility. The essential experience of art—one of them, anyway—is the sense of one time speaking to another. If it turns out that in truth the poems we're reading are essentially by contemporary Americans, we rightly feel tricked, and spooked. We're not surprised to find something contemporary that has contemporary values.

Of course, we can choose to shrug off the fraudulence and enjoy the poems as modern poems for their own sake. But when we do, we're engaging in a conscious policy of admission and acceptance. We know what we're doing and why. Communication is always two-way, sender and receiver, neither passive in the act. Messages sent are different from those received; messages received different from those sent. Recognizing this, aesthetic theorists warn us against the "intentional fallacy" and say not to pay exclusive attention to intention. But if we don't pay attention to intention, we don't know what we're missing. Intention is not everything in poetry or card sharking. But if we disregard intention, our response to the rest may go very wrong.

When we think about the intention and identity of the performer—or of a card cheat, or of a Persian poet—the trap is to get the wrong picture of the constraints and possibilities the performer or poet worked within. It isn't that it matters that much *which* Andrews is Erdnase. It's that if, as Forte strenuously argues, we have the wrong *kind* of Erdnase in mind, we're getting the wrong message from 1902. If, as Forte insists, Erdnase is not a world-weary card shark who has escaped to writing (!) as a means to make money, then our fixed picture of the constraints on a card manipulator in 1902 dissolves. Instead of a picture of world-weary card sharks cynically writing on magic tricks to broaden their appeal, we have one of brutal cheats who don't give a damn about expertise on the one hand, and of wistful wannabes who dress up on the page in the accepted familiar language of the con man to pass as glamorous on the other. A credible, but a different and less romantic, world. Just as, with Rumi, it seems we actually have less a Sufi Leonard Cohen and more a dutifully pious Muslim mystic with occasional glimmers of something more. The picture may be less pleasing, but it has the small, significant benefit of being true.

———

AT THE CORE of the mystery is a lesson we can too easily miss. It has to do with the way one time talks to another. We talk about things we prize, art above all, as "timeless." It's the most familiar generalization we make: it's a timeless picture, a timeless melody, or even a timeless card move. It's the highest praise we have.

But if we think about it, what we actually mean is not that something is "timeless" in the sense of transcendentally outside time. We mean just the opposite. We mean it's so deeply lodged within a time, and yet still so capable of speaking to our needs and experience, that there's something, well, masterly, not to say magical, about it.

There are countless things that *are* timeless in the sense of transcendentally outside time: simple machines, rules of thumb. The wheel is a timeless invention. But when we praise the wheel and the wheelmaker, we mean something very different from when we praise Shakespeare as a timeless writer or Michelangelo as a timeless draftsman or Erdnase as a timeless teacher of card manipulation. There we mean, actually, just the opposite of what we mean when we praise the timeless wheel and its unknown artisan. We mean they're so rooted in a time, so locked into a period, a tone, that we have to learn and relearn that tone in order to understand the time it comes from. And as we do, our own time appears. We recognize a work of art, with pleasure, as archaic or antique, only to find ourselves rewarded when it is still able to speak directly to our experience. By "timeless" in that sense, we don't mean outside time. We mean in two times at once: ours and theirs.

What we want from wheels is surely timelessness, but what we want from art *is* time, time leaping into time. Works of art are windows that have our time on one side, and another time when we look out. We love Erdnase because he is so delightfully dated, and yet his stilted sentences convey their truths. Wheels keep rolling, indifferent, from one epoch to another; works of art, high or low or in-between, are entirely inflected by their time, locked into one place at one moment and yet applicable to our own. Wheels roll; windows open.

Erdnase reaches young magicians not because they necessarily learn the work but because they learn the attitude, which is imprinted in his style as much as in his moves. As Darwin Ortiz says, "Techniques change but principles do not..." Erdnase's are: be cautious, careful, exact, precise, natural, and have an ironic understanding of what you're doing. That's the attitude the shape of his sentences imply. The naturalism is implicit in the whole.

———

THE PUNCH LINE of the story lies in what comes next in Forte's book. Though not a magician, and always anxious to separate himself from magic, he "closes" with more than two hundred pages of what he calls, delightfully, "Pseudo Gambling Stunts"—that is, card tricks. The real irony is that Forte has written, a century later, *exactly* the same book that he finds hard to imagine that Erdnase could have written a century before: a compendium of super-sharp and difficult gambling moves— with the proviso that gamblers, while cheating, don't often use them—plus a lot of magic stuff that is well to one side of his professional concerns but that he thinks, apologetically, is amusing to perform. Forte's book is a combination of the urge to come clean and the desire to entertain, given extra energy by the push-and-pull complexities of "disclosure," *there's so much I can do I can't say!* all narrated with the restless intelligence of a master who feels the universal human need to show off what he's mastered. Intentionally or not, he may be more eloquently explaining Erdnase's intention, and with it, his identity, than anyone ever has before.

Driving

I DECIDED TO LEARN TO DRIVE BECAUSE I WANTED to learn to drive. I wasn't, I told anyone who would listen, searching for a metaphor of middle age, or declaring my emancipation from my pedestrian past, or making up for time wasted in the passenger seat. There's a rich literature about learning to drive written by women, for whom it represents a larger emancipation from the feminine roles of enforced passivity, of sitting in place and accepting helplessness. That wasn't my "issue." I wanted to learn to drive because I wanted to make a vehicle move in an orderly direction forward and around corners and to necessary places.

I didn't know how to drive for reasons that seemed to me obvious and accidental and psychologically uncomplicated. My parents, who worked a few blocks from our apartment, didn't have a car for a few brief years that happened to coincide with my teenage ones. Then, in my early twenties, I found myself in New York, where people don't have cars, and where, among a thousand enterprises in transportation, from learning to roller-skate to mastering the transfer from the 6 train to the R to get to Times Square, taking the time to learn to drive seemed the least worthwhile. The years, and the decades, had flown past, and on that once-a-year summer occasion when we rented a car and set off for Cape Cod, my wife, Martha, who grew up in a semi-suburb of Montreal and had her license at eighteen, did the driving. She was a terrific, expert, careful driver, and the last thing we seemed to need in the family was another. I simply wanted to be her relief chauffeur—a middle-inning guy, able to go to the pond on an August morning or to the drive-in movie theater on an August evening. I wanted to be able to get ice cream at night and cinnamon buns in the morning.

Of course, there were other, more ignoble motives pressing on the decision to learn. Even as a feminist in a feminist age, I sometimes felt that I was in the wrong seat. Instead of sitting where generations of fathers have sat, pressing down on pedals and cursing the competition on the road, I had spent decades in the traditional mother's seat, filling her role—shushing the children when the driver was tired or looking for the exit, or holding out the paper bag of cookies to unseen, waiting hands in the back. When the rental-car man or the gas-station attendant approached the driver's seat and saw me in the "wrong" one, I immediately glared and scowled in what I imagined to be a persuasive imper-sonation of a hugely overskilled driver, the kind whose license has finally been taken away by the cops, however reluctantly, after a lifetime of dangerous but entertaining high-speed, *Dukes of Hazzard*–like performance. (Though I accept that these gender roles are nine-tenths "constructed," invented, and cast, still that does not make it less of a temptation to play another: that the clown wants to play Hamlet does not mean he thinks the actor playing Hamlet is actually a prince.)

My immediate trigger, though, was simpler: my son, Luke, turning twenty, had to get *his* license—he was a sophomore at a liberal-arts college just out of town—and various Robert Bly–Iron John–type scenarios of manhood achieved and passed on still existed somewhere in the Walter Mitty theater of my mind. "Let's learn to drive together," I said. But where, in the typical contemporary memoir, the troubled youth and the alienated father would silently acknowledge their vexed journey toward mastery and adulthood, he merely gave me an opaque look and asked if I was really sure this was a good idea, and had I run it by Mom? "Your reflexes are a bit funny, Dad," he said. I made a joke about being guys together, he mumbled something about "gender fluidity," which he had been studying in college, and we agreed to go to the Department of Motor Vehicles together and take the test for learner's permits.

The DMV has become such a byword for bureaucratic indifference and big-government horrors that it was nice to discover that the 125th Street branch, at least, was about as well run a place as one could hope to find. As we waited, I insisted that the reason government bureaus could seem so bureaucratic was that, by their nature, they have to be inclusive, and they can't inflict the basic market rationale of price differences upon their customers. If the privileged could pay more for quicker service, they would, but this would undermine the premises of citizenship. That first-class passengers get a shorter line through security claws at our idea of citizenship, which ought to include the notion that the rich and the poor suffer the indignities and delays of common civic cause equally. That this has never happened—the rich could buy their way out of Civil War conscription—doesn't make it less of an ideal. I want Charles Koch waiting in line alongside his chauffeur to be checked for hidden bombs and razors.

I was talking too much, and too quickly, because I was nervous beyond words about the test. I hadn't taken a test in many decades, and I was afraid that I hadn't studied the little booklet of road rules well enough. People do fail the written test, and in New York state more than half of those who take the road test fail that one. "Dad, it's easy—it's multiple choice," Luke said as we waited to enter the test-taking room. "There will be two answers that are obviously wrong. Then there will be two sort of plausible ones. If you just choose the plausible ones at random you'll get fifty percent. Since you do know *something*, you'll get more than half of that right for sure. You can't help passing." The American social truth—that what we spend years teaching our children is essentially to spot the two obviously wrong answers—was the essential truth of the DMV too. The larger social truth Luke was touching on, that being good at passing tests has relatively little to do with being good at what those tests are supposed to be testing, in the end came to haunt my entire experience of learning to drive.

I passed the test and got my permit, with a suitably grim photograph, and the very next week I signed up with a driving school in Manhattan that was supposed to be particularly good with later-in-life students. At five thirty on a Tuesday afternoon, I got into the driver's seat of a car parked outside my apartment building and advertised on the side as "Student Driver." I noticed that various catchphrases had been laboriously written out in block letters on adhesive tape and stuck to the dashboard: "NOODLES!!!" and "BUSY BEE!!!" and "GSSLG!"

"I love it, yuuusss, I *love* it!" Arturo Leon, my driving instructor, said with more enthusiasm than I expected as I adjusted my mirrors, trying to recall how my father had always aligned these things. And then, to my shock—I expected to be eased into the pool, inch by inch—he had me pull out into the street and make a left turn on the adjoining avenue, and there I was—at rush hour on the Upper East Side, heading north among impatient taxicabs, doing what I suppose was a steady, frightened fifteen miles an hour while the world roared and bleated around me, speeding past our little car. Arturo, I noticed, kept his foot alarmingly well away from the extra brake on his side in the specially prepared student car.

Panic enveloped me. Taxis were honking furiously—furious, I dimly realized, at me! "Let's give him the hand," Arturo said, showing me a gentle, palm-out wave. "Just give him the hand: 'Yes, thank you for sharing.'" He was addressing the car alongside us as its driver yelled soundlessly. He smiled. We moved forward up the avenue. Driving was like a nightmare, or, rather, like a dream I had had many times at the age of six or seven, of being behind the wheel of my father's car and moving forward, floating forward. I broke out in a sweat—up Madison into the South Bronx, incredibly doing this thing.

Though I kept my eyes mostly pointed rigidly ahead, in the moments when we stopped at a red light ("I want to see the floor under the car ahead of us," Arturo would instruct me, and it took me a while to understand that by "floor" he meant the asphalt street surface; that, a city boy like me, he thought that everything flat and low on the ground *was* a floor), I got to study my teacher. Cherub-faced and immense, he worked nights as a DJ with his brother, loved to sing scraps of old Motown songs as we drove, and thought that rush-hour Manhattan and the crowded shopping streets of Arthur Avenue and Third Avenue in the South Bronx, where he lived, were the perfect arena for learning to drive. As I drove, struggling to keep the terror down, Arturo kept up a nonstop patter. He was a great teacher and a champion talker, somehow managing to be both elaborately formal—he couched any direction, even a last-minute, life-saving one, as a

polite request—and cheerily intimate: I learned about his Ecua-
dorean parentage and his immigrant upbringing, his failed marriage, his two beloved children, and his future prospects, both
erotic and professional.

"OK, we're going uptown, please continue straight ahead—
excellent," he would say casually, hissing the *xc*. And then: "I
love it!" We would head north to approach the Madison Avenue
Bridge, or the Willis Avenue Bridge, or the Third Avenue
Bridge—all bridges of which I had previously been entirely
unaware. "Do I turn here?" I would say, my voice shaky, as liv-
ery drivers and cabbies raced around and ahead of me. "If you
would just push the car slightly left just here?" he would reply.
"Just slide over. Just *slide* into the left lane. Just look and signal
and *sliiide*. Thank you! Thank you! Excellent. I'm so happy with
the way you did that." He started to sing: "*Because I'm happy
/ Clap along if you feel like a room without a roof. / Because I'm
happy / Clap along if you feel like happiness is the truth.*" And then:
"Thank you for doing that so easily. And we'll just continue
here, and now I'm going to stop you *here*." He nimbly slipped
his foot sideways onto his own brake, as, coming off the bridge
at my steady fifteen miles per hour, I narrowly missed a sixteen-
wheeler coming the other way. The truck driver blasted his
horn—his steam siren, really—and Arturo waved gently at him.
"Let's give him the hand, right here," he said. "The hand means
thank you, bless you, fuck you. The hand means everything we
need it to mean. Oh, thank you so much for signaling to us! Sharing is caring!" He would smile serenely while slipping in through
his smile an obscenity directed at the truck driver for my benefit,
and I would laugh and give the truck driver the hand too. Then
Arturo would lean back and let me drive while he told me about
his kids—Bryan Armany and Hillary Alizé—and his struggles

to keep them in a straight line at school, about his father's bad health and his mother's love.

"Become the noodle!" he kept insisting, and I soon learned that this meant to relax completely, go limp from head to toe. His constant talk, I decided, was intended to *make* you become the noodle by not allowing you to think too much. Dread is always the product of imagination. You see the bad consequence coming and the image paralyzes your judgment. Arturo had me on the FDR Drive at rush hour before I had a chance to think about it.

Two or three times a week, we would spend a couple of hours driving, up to the South Bronx and back again. (Luke did five hours, and it was a wrap: he was ready for the road test.) Arturo would have me crawl along Arthur Avenue and Third Avenue, learning the complicated timing necessary to avoid pedestrians crossing against the light, and then go out into the empty, boarded-over areas of the borough to practice parallel parking and three-point turns. Then he would reward me by taking me out onto one of the big highways, the Bruckner or the FDR, where I could, unbelievably, go forty miles an hour and negotiate lanes like a cabbie, until I found the exit home.

Unlike drawing, unlike doing magic at least by proxy, driving seemed at first to negate the usual path of learning: the incremental steps, the breaking down and building up of parts, the curve we go up as one small mastery follows another. Driving, I realized, isn't really difficult; it's just extremely dangerous. You hit the gas and turn the wheel, and there you are—in possession of a two-ton weapon capable of being pointed at anything you like, at any speed you can go at, just by pressing a pedal a little bit harder. The poor people in the crosswalk—the guy in the tank top striding indifferently forward; the mother yanking at her child's hand—had no idea of the danger they were in with me behind the wheel! *I* had no idea of the danger I am in doing the same thing, day after day. Cars are terrifying, and cars are normality itself.

This discrepancy between difficulty and danger is our civilization's signature, from machine guns to atomic bombs. You press a pedal and two tons of metal lurches down the city avenue; you pull a trigger and twenty enemies die; you waggle a button and cities burn. The point of living in a technologically advanced society is that minimal effort can produce maximal results. Making hard things easy is the path to convenience; it is also the lever of catastrophe. The realization of how close to disaster we were at every moment helped press my panic button, and while Arturo's singing and commentary reduced the panic some, I tried to find other ways to overcome it as well.

———

ONE WAY TO calm myself was to become my calm father. Whenever I think of him, I am in the backseat and I see the back of his head, his mesh driving gloves, and his calm voice debating a topic with his children improbably crowded in behind him. (My first memories of life are in the Volkswagen Bug my parents bought in the late '50s, into whose tiny backseat they introduced, like clowns into a clown car, one child after another, until there were six.) To see him so is to do a terrible disservice to his accomplishments—a chauffeur is the last thing he was—and yet in another way it is to see him whole, if one translates the act of driving into an act of understated service. He thought little of doing a kind of drive-around of his six children and twelve grandchildren, now dispersed around the continent like pieces on a game board. From rural Ontario to Boston to Ann Arbor to Berkeley to Washington to New York—the driving would last fifteen or sixteen hours, and he would emerge, bearded and smiling. "I've never had an accident," he liked to say. We were very close when I was a teenager, and I loved him more for knowing that I was not remotely like him: he was sound, solid, in his role as a dean paterfamilias to a campus—all things I never hoped to be. My not driving was, in some sense, a response to his driving all the time. We make ourselves in our father's sunlight but also in his shadow: what he beams down we bend away from.

He had been driving, he often recalled, since he was twelve, as a young boy on a farm in Montgomery County, Pennsylvania, his family, unusually, Jews among the Pennsylvania Dutch. He first drove an army-surplus jeep, used as a tractor, and at sixteen got his license. He often told me of how, as a teenager, having a car was the means not just to autonomy—though it was that: you could get behind the wheel and go to Atlantic City, to Provincetown, even to old Quebec—but to privacy. It enabled a lower-middle-class kid in a fractious, noisy extended family to be alone with his thoughts. He said to me once, when I was small, "You know, you can drive right across the country now without a stoplight." The image stayed with me. (I suspect that the significant things we say to our children usually vanish, while incidental oddities linger.) I wanted to travel with him, but I left the driving to him.

Why, I wondered, had he never encouraged me to drive? Why had he not kept a car when I was a teenager? He gave me a driving lesson once—in Italy on a sabbatical leave, as it happened—and it had gone all right. But then he stopped, and he didn't really have to; we didn't have a car, that was true, but there were friends and rentals. If driving mattered so much to him, why would it not to me? Had he failed me in some way, or had I failed him in some way I was still not ready to recognize?

LEARNING TO DRIVE changed my perception of the city. Premodern peoples have to be persuaded that what they impute to sapient agency is actually the work of automatic forces: lightning, tides, the moon rising are not the result of gods or demons working their will but just things that happen from consciousnessless natural forces. I had to persuade myself that what I had grown to attribute to automatic forces was actually the work of agency. The crazy taxi driver, weaving in and out of traffic, I had always viewed with what was, to my wife, undue calm—he was like a whirlpool in the river's flow, just what was happening naturally. That he was *making* it happen, and should not have been, was not a thought entirely at home in my head. It had never occurred to me that the pulse and movement of traffic was not like the eddies and currents of rivers but a network of decisions made at frantic high speeds by cooperative and conflicting drivers. The deeper truth was that I accepted the action of cars as automatic forces because I thought, in effect, that my father was driving them all. I had always so trusted him up there in the front seat, as a benevolent natural force, that I extended that trust to anyone in that place.

This opacity of agency in car driving, and the ways we try to surmount it, turns out to be the subject of intense academic study. Distilling an argument from my reading, most of which was created under the general aegis of the studies of street traffic done by the sociologist Erving Goffman, I had the sense that it all seemed to intersect on the idea that we regard cars as shells, closed homes, more than as mobile weapons. Traffic is a way of avoiding looking at other people's faces. We like being in cars because they give us my father's teenage illusion of privacy, and as a consequence we are unduly surprised and even enraged when we are reminded that there are other people like us in them. Road rage is a function of mind blindness induced by the car's enclosure: when we're locked in our car's little confession box, it's easy to arrive at the illusion that we're the only person out there. We consistently underrate the movements of cars as intentional objects, and then, in an instant, overrate them. A vehicle that obstructs our way is first a mute object in the maze to be avoided and then, suddenly, a menace. This is why the driver acting erratically, unexpectedly pulling ahead, or moseying down Madison at fifteen miles per hour prompts "You idiot!" rather than "Are you OK?"

Arturo's method, assuming that there was one, was, in part, to make driving a car more like walking on a sidewalk, full of recognitions and hand waving and early avoidance, tamping down the sudden shocks that the combustion engine is heir to. Driving so much with Arturo after reading the academics, I not only began to enjoy it but also began to like cars, and to see that driving is one of the last democratic things we do. I had long thought of cars as a weapon against civilization, and had said as much many times in print. They devoured cities, destroyed mass transit, assaulted walkers, greedily demanded parking lots where once there had been public space, and, worst of all, sent families out from dense cities into atomized suburbs. But now I saw that driving was in another way civilization itself: self-organizing, self-controlling, a pattern of agreement and coalition made at high speed and, on the whole, successfully. "Just signal and slide over," Arturo would urge me on the highway, and, as I signaled, other cars—other drivers—actually let me slide over! No cop appeared at the edge of the road to enforce the rule. They just did! Swerving and sliding over is citizenship, and the startling thing is how commonplace and easy it is. It was the essential social contract at work at forty miles an hour. The arrival of the self-driving car, though it might make the world easier for non-drivers like me—and, given how little I was improving, I thought it quite possible that I would remain a non-driver for life—would still mark a loss in courtesy. "Sharing is caring," Arturo would sing out, again and again, and though he meant it somewhat sardonically, he also really meant it: we were sharing the public road, and that alone was a way of caring for our fellow drivers. Arturo's all-purpose hand—the one that means "thank you," "fuck you," "who cares about you"—is the proper hand for a citizen. It broadcast civility while keeping its private meanings to itself.

Along the way, Arturo tried to explain to me what he wanted me to do to prepare for the road test that Luke and I had scheduled together for late October. Tactfully, he tried to get me to see that my job was not just to show that I could turn corners and do three-point turns and parallel park. More, it was to impress the license-giving tester with my readiness to do anything that was required of me, and to do it in a suitably deferential spirit. "They make their decision in the first ten seconds," he explained, over and over. "In the first *five* seconds, just by looking at you. They want to see you work the mirrors, they want to see you check your blind spot—they want to see you *work* your blind spot." He showed me how I needed to behave: twisting my neck around in the car to look over my shoulder, my neck bobbing back and forth inside my collar, like Rodney Dangerfield doing standup for an audience in the backseat.

I complained that I saw what was behind me more clearly if I just faced front and looked in the rearview mirrors. "I know," he said, sighing. "It doesn't matter. You got to be the busy bee anyway! They make up their mind in the *first* second they look at you— it's up to you to show them that you are a safe, skillful, and secure driver by the way you behave when you start up the car, even before you move an inch." He gave me a brief, dispassionate breakdown of the character of the driving judges, who were joined together by pride of office. They liked skill, but they hated arrogance. They wanted *humble* drivers. As Luke had explained to me that the key to the written exam was that it was multiple choice, Arturo was telling me that the key to the road test was that it was *not* multiple choice, it was a game of Simon Says, call and response. The point was to figure out exactly what the tester wanted and then do it.

Over time, Arturo and I became friendly, exchanging confidences about our kids—we both had a boy and a girl, his daughter Hillary named admiringly after Mrs. Clinton, while his son, Bryan Armany, like mine, Luke Auden, had a first name he liked the sound of and the middle name of an artist he admired. We talked a lot about the difficulties of fathering: when to press hard on the gas, when to let up—when to be present and when to recede. He was in the middle of managing his father's decline, in and out of hospitals, moments of lucidity rising in a mire of confusion.

One evening, as I dodged the pedestrians in the South Bronx, or they dodged me, Arturo turned toward me. "Adam, I have something I want to ask you."

"Sure, Arturo, what?" He seemed so formal.

"How do you write a book?" he said. "There's a book I have in mind. It's called 'Dream Driving,' all about my way of teaching driving. How you have to think about driving when you're not in the car. How you have to be the busy bee. How you have to shift gear, steer, signal, look, go." That was what that "GSSLG" on his dashboard meant. "How you have to *dream* about driving to drive well. How do you write a book like that?"

Writing a book seemed as mysterious a process to him, one as much in need of elaborate advance and afterthought, as driving a car was to me. The secret to both—that, really, you sort of just do it—seemed as inadequate an answer to his question as it would have been to any of mine. I stumbled out something about making an outline, thinking through what you wanted to say, making sure that your sentences on the page sounded a little like your voice in life.

"You sort of get better at it the more you write," I said. "You have to just keep writing and then, I promise, it will start to feel easier as you do it."

He paused. "You become the noodle?" he said.

Yes, I agreed. You have to become the noodle to write a book. For the only moment in our time together, he didn't say anything at all.

———

THE DAY OF the road test arrived at last, and I drove all the way to Bronxville, Arturo in the seat beside me, to collect Luke. The tests were being given in a residential neighborhood not far from there.

Any prospect for father-son bonding in road anxiety was quickly dispelled by Luke. "I'm just glad I'm not going to have to come back here after I get my license," he said. There was no doubt at all in his mind that he was going to get it.

I took the exam first. The examiner got into the car beside me. She was a tiny African American woman who sank down into the seat, barely coming up to the level of the windshield. She told me briefly to pull out and make a left turn. I did.

"Why are you so nervous?" she asked me impatiently. "What's making you nervous?"

My soul sank. Was it that obvious? This was getting off to a terrible start.

"The circumstance," I answered, dry-mouthed.

"*What* circumstance? Make a left turn at the light."

"The circumstance of taking a test," I said.

Oddly, that seemed to please her. "Well," she said. Then: "How can you not have a license? How can you *never* have had a license? Where did you grow up?"

I guided the car at what I hoped was the right pace along the streets and gave her the whole story. She had me park and do the three-point turn. Then she had me pull over.

"What are *you* going to do with a license?" she demanded.

I smiled weakly. "Take my kids to the ocean," I said at last.

"What ocean? You're going to the damned *Hamptons*?" Her tone was one of amused disdain: she could see right through me to the other side of the street.

"No," I said. "Cape Cod."

"Cape Cod! I like Martha's Vineyard."

"Why?" I came back. I sensed that she wanted me to.

"Why?" she answered. "It reminds me of down south."

"Yes, it does," I said sapiently. "There's a certain resemblance in the foliage . . ."

"When have you ever been down south?"

I smiled weakly again. She asked me what I did for a living. I told her I wrote.

"I could write a book," she said.

"What about?"

"This!" It was so obvious. "What people do on driving tests."

"Well, tell me one good story that would go in a book," I said. She wanted a little resistance, I felt, some nerve shown from the student.

"There's a million," she said, and she began to work her little handheld computer. After a while, she asked, again, "What are you going to do with this license?"

My heart leaped as I realized that she was going to give it to me. I was going to be a licensed driver! But her puzzlement was real. Her tone was that of a bureaucrat being asked to provide a marriage certificate to a hospice patient; she could supply the paper, but she could not really see the point.

"I'm going to drive home," I said at last.

She snorted. There was an odd mixture of hostility and good humor in her conversation—with enough class and race and sexual politics implicit in it to supply several seminar rooms at Luke's liberal-arts college. She had taken my measure within the first ten seconds: no great shakes as a driver, but desperately eager to do well; responsible, if a little ridiculous; no danger on the road to the good people of New York state. It turned out that I had made two mistakes on the road test—taken too wide a left turn, and not signaled when I pulled out from my parallel-parking space. Still, if I was willing to be deferential, she was prepared to be decently tolerant of my absurdity. If I would be the noodle, she would be the sauce.

When I got out of the car, clutching my little piece of paper, Arturo embraced me, and we jumped up and down like a pitcher and catcher after the last out of the World Series. "I knew you could do it! I knew it! I knew it!" He seemed almost as excited as I was.

I called my dad, in Canada. (Luke, of course, got his license one-two-three, just like that.) He was pleased but didn't seem particularly impressed. "The important thing is that now you know how to drive," he said. "I'm seventy-nine, and I got my license when I was sixteen and I've never had an accident."

Now you know how to drive—the simple monosyllables hovered in the air. Knowing how to drive is part of knowing how to live. Everyone has a role: we yield, scoot, slide, wave, nod, sigh, deny each other space, and give each other license.

The amazing thing is that, while it sometimes ends up in a horrible pileup, it doesn't *always* end up in a horrible pileup. That's civilization.

I put the license away in my wallet and didn't use it for several motionless months. We usually expand our capacities without changing our lives. People go off to meditation retreats and come back to their Manhattan existence; on the whole, they are not more serene, but they are much more knowing about where serenity might yet be found. People go to cooking school and don't cook more; but they know how to cook. Samuel Johnson was once asked why he always rushed to look at the spines of books in the library when he arrived at a new house. "Sir, the reason is very plain," he said. "Knowledge is of two kinds. We know a subject ourselves, or we know where we can find information upon it." Almost all of our useful knowledge is potential knowledge.

The potentials may serve merely as vicarious experience, but almost all experience is vicarious: that's why we have stories and movies and plays and pictures. It's why we have drive-in movies in summer towns. We expand our worlds through acts of limited empathy more than through plunges into unexpected places. My father's "Now you know how to drive" had wisdom buried in its simplicity. The highlights of life are first unbelievably intense and then absurdly commonplace. I am now a licensed driver. But almost everybody is a licensed driver. Having a child born is a religious experience. But everybody has kids. Everybody drives, and now I can too. That's all, and enough. Now I can drive straight across the country, without a stoplight. I don't think I ever will. But at least I know I can.

There is a postscript to the story. My father called in early January to say that, on the eve of his eightieth birthday, he had been forced to take a driving test.

"But it wasn't a driving test," my mother interrupted, not for the first time in their sixty-some years together.

"I'm getting there," he said, sounding unusually testy with her. It had been a very Canadian test, he explained, a vision examination allied to a reading test, conducted in a friendly spirit—but its dagger end was present. One of the eighty-year-olds tested had had his license taken away, never to drive again. Social life involves being sorted by a few others who have, by the rest of us, been given the power to sort. Our illusion is that it ends on graduation, from one school or another, when one teacher passes us, and then passes us on. But it never really does. We go on being driven and sorted, until at last we're sorted out, and driven home.

———

SINCE GETTING MY LICENSE, I've become a regular driver, though I'm still not a *good* driver, let alone anything resembling what one would think is a master driver—a racecar driver or stunt driver, for instance. But the way in which the process of driving seemed to evade the usual process of slow, dumb parts coalescing into a seamless intelligent practice was only a superficial insight. With driving, the practice is not in learning to manipulate the car. It lies in learning incrementally how *not* to recognize the reality of what we're doing when we manipulate a car. Every driver, or just about every driver, becomes a master in this sense. If we had ever, as a society, accurately calculated the risks and costs of the individual car—if we had recognized the mutilation and death and crippling that would result every year from the mad act of letting minimally skilled Americans drive tons of steel at high speeds with no effective supervision— we would never have allowed cars in the first place. The same calculations of risk with airplanes or trains have led to incomparably more rigorous standards of licensing. The mastery of driving lies less in learning to see and steer than in learning, step by step, to be selectively blind, prudently indifferent. One form of mastery is the mastery of not seeing too much.

The Third Mystery
of Mastery

The Hummingbird's Heartbeat, or,
The Mystery of Interiority

B Y NOW, YOU HAVE HEARD THE RUMOR: THE hummingbird and the whale have the same number of heartbeats in a lifetime, differently expended. In that truth we seek some consolation for the speed of our mortality. Each being has a heart that beats a billion times—one over months, the other over decades. The hummingbird lives a brief and busy life, its heart beating literally a thousand times a minute, and the whale a slow and ponderous existence out in the deep. Yet their inner experience, the heartbeat rhythm of their lives, is foundationally alike. The hummingbird would not trade its place for the whale's, because the hummingbird's life *is* the whale's, in a decent existential translation. Just as Mozart was writing his late work— purified, simplified, the essence of his melodic genius—when he was still in his thirties, the hummingbird enjoys the fruits of youth at one week, the wisdom of old age at thirty-two months.

The deeper question this rumor raises is about the limits our carnality puts on our capacities. What *can't* we do, because we aren't designed to do it? As much as anything else, it is the physical limitations of being human that shapes our approach to the real work. This is true in ways both small—break a finger and you will not be able to fret your guitar—and large: for the first part of our lives we grow, then we begin to age, and while growth carries with it the potential of learning, age is inevitably bound up with things discarded. We stoop, we bend, we break, we gasp for breath, and our shiny visions of doing anew and making over run up routinely against the brick-and-cement wall of fact. There's a lot we simply can't do, and not just the obvious physical stuff that leaves the happy jogger dead of a heart attack at fifty and the older woman with the face lift looking only like an older woman with a face lift. The limit affects our inner accomplishments, too, as names become harder to find and the inequities of life become more piercing in their entry into our lives.

In the face of that uncompromising physicality, we search for some kind of heart's ease, a *hope*, and one way we find it is to insist that there are secret solvents of the injustice of our interiors, of our plumbing and construction and the sell-by date imprinted on our genome. One hope lies in the odd connection between— literally, as kids say—the insides of our heads and the beatings of our hearts. The limits on our accomplishments may be constrained by our plumbing and our heating; there may be only so many heartbeats to go around. But if our *consciousness* of our heartbeats is shaped by our own internal clocks, why, we might partake of one common oceanic swell of life. With every creature sentenced alike to a billion heartbeats, we can choose how to expend them—quickly in a fever of work, like Mozart or Townes Van Zandt, or slowly, like Methuselah and Willie Nelson. Mozart lost his heartbeats quickly in the cause of music; Methuselah spent his heartbeats slowly, for some strange patriarchal purpose.

The tragedy of mortality might be, if not evaded, then at least eased as inner experience. Though our public incapacity and decline may be inescapable, our private experience of pleasure and existence may be in itself a leveling force. Our interior experience of accomplishment and mastery matter. They may even matter most of all. We lost the public race to be the best long ago; the inequities of circumstance and of the complicated thing called talent may have put us permanently in the rear. But the last runner need compete only with herself. Her heartbeats are well expended even in the loss. I take as much pleasure from playing "Lullaby of Birdland" badly as George Shearing did in writing it well. Use Your Heartbeats! cries the Internet meme, and as poet Mary Oliver wrote, we can at least choose how to spend them, decide what is it you plan to do with your own wild and precious life.

———

IT IS THE kind of thing that seems unknowable but, in fact, can be known. It turns out that there is a whole research project devoted to the study of the variety of heartbeats, from hummingbird to human, at North Carolina State University, where, under the direction of a visionary of "citizen science" named Rob Dunn, a handful of ingenuous researchers decided to find out how many heartbeats each creature actually has. Instead of counting all the heartbeats themselves, they realized that they could turn to the citizens, the public, and ask them to send in whatever heartbeats they had counted. It's the kind of research that would have delighted Darwin, who spent his rich, later years organizing small-scale experiments on actual living things in his dining room, including forming an "Earthworm Octet" with his children in order to detect if earthworms—which were to the later Darwin what clarinet and chamber music were to the (unknowingly later) Mozart, the perfect means for a purification of purpose—could hear music. (They couldn't.) The heartbeat project, which Dunn has passed on to his student Clint Penick, now at Kennesaw State, is the purification of purpose for the North Carolina scientists. Drawing on a spectrum of sources—many public, some private, some old and some new—by now they have counted heartbeats from 176 species of mammals, 60 species of birds, 40 species of reptiles, and 41 species of fish.

And what have they found? Lauren Nichols, one of the scientists on the project—whose usual research specialty includes the study of the evolution of sourdough yeasts, and who has the winning habit of referring to obscure animals whose heartbeats she has studied but whose scientific names she can't for the moment recall as "whatchamacallits," as in "It's one of those weird Australian whatchamacallits"—sums up what they set out to find, and what they found after they set out.

"Everyone was saying that there's a close correlation between heart rate and length of life, from monkeys to cats to dogs. But it made us ask: What kind of monkey? What kind of dog? We realized that the data must exist, over the past century, in a million separate unrelated inquiries, but had never been compiled because it was never thought of as something important enough to put in a paper. So, we took advantage of the truth that ordinary people are really good sleuths and are interested in participating and put out a call for heartbeats. We wanted to take a common truth and see if it was true. That sentiment was all over the Internet, but science finds out when it's true and when it's not true.

"By now we have a bunch of mammals—there are, like, five thousand known mammals, and we have more than one hundred and fifty so far. We don't have as a good data set for birds, only have about sixty . . . and of course reptiles and fishes are more infrequently, um, held up for heartbeat counts." (How *do* you put a stethoscope to a rhesus monkey or robin redbreast?

"It's a problem. Because most of the time, measurements are made on either an animal that has been sedated, which slows their heart rate, or an animal that's alert and anxious because they are being handled by humans, and their hearts are beating faster than usual. We need to put an asterisk against any of these outliers.")

"But as the real numbers have come in—on average, and averages always mask the truth—it really does seem to be true that life averages out around a billion beats. Some species break the mold, in either direction. Looking really quick at the data, you see that the Southern Brown Bandicoot, that's an Australian fauna marsupial, looks a little bit like a whatchamacallit—you know, like an opossum—it gets less than three hundred million, and so it has a pretty short life-span of six and a half years, even though it has a resting heart rate of eighty-four beats per minute. Closer to humans are red-faced spider monkeys—they have *really* fast heartbeats, two hundred and seventy beats per minute, and they can live around forty-six years, while a Brush-Tailed Phascogale—that's another Australian whatchamacallit—has two hundred and ten heartbeats per minute and can live for around six years. They have very similar heartbeats, and vastly different life-spans. Why? This is the kind of question that we can answer when we have enough data to do an analysis of mammals: are species closely related to each other similar in heartbeat and life-span, or does it have more to do with other questions of geographic distribution?

"One thing for certain we, as humans, are the top of the chain: if we get really old, we have the potential to get to *five billion beats*, though that's probably mostly true because of modern medicine. We doubt that that's genetic—but we don't know, cross-culturally. One theory is that your heart is a muscle and can't regenerate, and there's a certain number of times it can beat before it wears itself out. Or maybe, this is another theory, heartbeats are only a local symptom of your metabolism: smaller animals have different surface-area ratio, so their metabolism is determined differently. But there's questions about species that fall outside of that metabolism measure that have fewer heartbeats than we expect. It's generally true that heartbeats are what we have, and most living things, us aside, have about the same number." Then, unbidden, she added: "It's like an experimental version of, you know, that Mary Oliver poem . . . You know, the one that ends, 'What is it you plan to do with your own wild and precious life?'" (Despite what they say about the end of literacy, some poems remain common property.)

Rob Dunn, the original director of the project, and of the lab, says: "It's never clear-clear. It's messy-clear. A billion heartbeats per lifetime, with the human exception, though that may be newly hatched from modern medicine. But the hummingbird and the whale? Yeah, *that's* true. The average hummingbird lives three to five years; one point three billion beats. At the opposite end, gray whales can live for seventy-seven years with twenty-eight beats per minute. One point one billion."

———

TO HOPE FOR this leveling truth between birds and whales is, of course, to impart to the bird (and the big fish) an inner life that is peculiarly human. If we were hummingbirds, would our lives feel to us as long and full as those of whales? After all, we have managed to articulate our lives in so many neatly rounded segments that they give the decent illusion of length: infancy, childhood, adolescence, maturity, middle age . . . why, the worst thing we know is a young person dying, because our lives, though still absurdly short by any standards, feel long enough, broken as they are into parts.

In his famous philosophical paper "What Is It Like to Be a Bat?" Thomas Nagel suggested that we cannot know what it is to be a bat, because if we were a bat ourselves, we would not *be* ourselves, not have our peculiar stream of memories, understandings, and specific self-consciousness. Being a bat, we would not know what it is like to be a bat. We can only imagine what it is like to be a human in a bat suit.

There is, as subsequent generations of critics have pointed out, a slippery substance inside this logic, tarnishing the silver of the argument. Following on the same logic, we could never know what it is like to be *anything* outside ourselves, since even if, in the natural logic of fantasy, we became our mother or brother or neighbor, we still would bring within that shell our own history, and thus be us—or else we would not, and, once again, could not, know what it is to like to be them. Indeed, the same logic would prevent us ever knowing what it is like to be *us*, since that, too, is a made-up, ever-shifting business—a truth that Buddha and David Hume alike suggest.

Yet if nature constrains us, it helps to know what those natural constraints really are. Nature gives us mixed consolations. Studying snowflakes, we were once told that they were all different, and thus gave some kind of natural metaphoric endorsement to our inherent individuality. Instead, it turns out that snowflakes are all alike, when they begin in clouds, changing in form and appearance only as they drift to earth through the accidents of wind and weather. A better image, that, of how we truly live and differentiate ourselves. So: do the hummingbirds' hearts beat as they're said to, or is it a pretty story hiding a darker physical truth, for example, that hummingbirds beat hard and briefly, then quit, while big, charismatic creatures get the heartbeats, the longevity, and eventually, the mates while the birds flutter over nectar briefly and then expire?

Is all experience equal? Is the well-fed bull as happy as the high-minded philosopher? (Dr. Johnson proposed this question, and answered, firmly, No!) The mystery of interiority may simply be that we are all hummingbirds, and we are all whales. But we are also quite possibly all brush-tailed phascogales and southern brown bandicoots. The constraints on our conditions are real, but far from absolute. We can be aware of our limits and still enjoy walking around the hortus conclusus, the hidden garden, God has given us. In fact, the constraints are often the springboard to accomplishment. Lose a finger and you lose the ability to fret—but lose *two* fingers, completely, as happened to the peerless jazz-manouche guitarist Django Reinhardt, and you invent a whole new system for playing chords.

The solution to the mystery of heartbeats is messy-clear, as truths tend to be. There is, yes, a permanent thrumming beat in the world, not quite audible, or not heard without help, that counts out again and again to a billion. If we could press our ears to the air and hear a billion heartbeats, overlapping, one new set ready to begin as another ends, the percussion of existence, the sound of life, would be audible, lulling in its regularity. Yet against that permanent rhythm come the little syncopations of our existence, and those off-beats, and extended beats, are our possibility and our permanence. Human beings have extra heartbeats, made perhaps by medicine, perhaps by metabolism. Still, faced with the fact of mortality, we do beat on.

So what Larger Lesson does the mutability of heartbeats leave for the real work? First, that what goes on inside our heads—how we feel about what we're doing—matters as much as what we actually get done. A hummingbird's life, like Mozart's, need not be experienced as an abbreviated one. An achieved life is achieved, not extended. And then the knowledge of our physical limits doesn't change only our capacity for things. It changes our *response* to things. I once asked, in an essay about artificial intelligence, for readers to imagine a chain of supercomputers that were wired to the fuse on an explosive that would, on a fixed date in the future, destroy them—and to imagine, too, that the information about the bomb was part of their programming. They would doubtless begin to do their processing double-time, quicken and aphorize their information, turn to compact myth and compressed drama instead of extended proofs to make their points. Everything they did would be haunted by the knowledge that they wouldn't be able to do it for very long.

Well, we are those computers. Our knowledge of our mortality, of our physical limits—of the number of heartbeats we've used and have left—infects and infests everything we do and make. And if this turns us anxious and panicky in some ways, it also makes us generous in other ways, more inclined to value the performance of mastery even when it's flawed, to see in frailty and imperfection not only the signs of life, as in the singer's vibrato, but the signs of the *limits* on life.

I suddenly think of the drum solos that we all used to dread at rock concerts, where the drummer would bash on for five excruciating extra minutes. Ringo Starr, greatest of drummers, whose regular Beatle beat has often been likened to a heartbeat, refused, until the very end of the Beatles, to play a solo. Until, in the end, in "The End," the last song on their last-recorded album, he stopped refusing, and declared himself, briefly but loudly, before sinking back into the band.

Human life, it seems, is the drum solo in the rock concert of animal existence: it's too loud, much too long by the standards of the other acts, and usually self-indulgent. No one except the player really enjoys it, even if it always gets a standing ovation when it's over. Yet would we really cheat the drummer of his solo? Even as we sigh and wait for the guitars and the song to begin again, we're happy for the affirmation. We're not glad to have heard it, but we're not sorry it happened. Plans may all fail, but doings don't. We get a standing ovation for having persisted. Or, perhaps, for being done.

Baking

THOUGH I AM A KITCHEN COOK, I HAVE NEVER been a home baker. For years, I told myself that I didn't bake bread for the same reason I didn't drive a car: it's a useful skill, unnecessary in New York. In New York, you don't drive because you can take the subway practically anywhere, and you don't have to bake bread because there are so many good bakeries. Even at the supermarket, there are baguettes from Tom Cat and cinnamon-raisin loaves from Orwashers and Eli's empire of sourdoughs.

Recently, though, I was going through heirlooms that had been left by my wife's ailing, ninety-three-year-old mother when she moved out of the family house in Montreal, and found a beautiful hand-lettered, framed recipe for something called Martha's Bread. It was a long, very '70s-looking recipe, sampler-like in style, with instructions and ingredients—including lecithin granules and millet and oats and honey—surrounded by a watercolor border of leaves and falling petals and pumpkins.

"Martha's Bread!" I cried. (Martha is my wife.) "When did you bake bread?" To say that I was incredulous doesn't capture it. One way to describe Martha is to say that she looks like a woman who has never had a loaf of bread named after her—perfumes, dresses, and dances, perhaps, but not oat-and-honey bread. *No Loaves* might be the title of her personal manifesto.

"When I was a teenager," she said. "I sewed all my own clothes and I baked all my own bread."

This puzzled me. I knew her in her teens, and she never baked bread. She didn't sew her own clothes, either, not that I could see. She ate matzos with bits of canned asparagus on top, and she dressed, beautifully, in Icelandic woolens and Kenzo dresses and lace-up boots. So I was genuinely curious to see what she looked like baking a loaf of bread. After many years of marriage, you tend to focus your curiosity not on the spectacular moments that might yet happen but on excavating the stranger, smaller ones that did: your partner punching down dough at sixteen. As Proust knew, all love depends not just on current infatuation but on retrospective jealousy; lacking a classy old lover, a Marquis de Norpois, to be jealous of, I was jealous of the men in Montreal health-food stores who had sold her millet and lecithin granules.

"So why don't you make your bread?" I asked.

"My bread's not that easy," she said loftily. "I have to get a big earthenware bowl to make this bread. And a big wooden breadboard. I used to have them at home. I used to make this bread with my friend Rachel. She's the one who illuminated the recipe. We would bake all day in aprons and then drink tea and eat our bread with honey." The thought of her in an apron surrounded by all that homey '70s blond wood was so intoxicating that, to shake the spell, I resolved to start on a loaf that night. I lighted upon the now legendary "No-Knead Bread" recipe I clipped from the *Times* some years ago. Invented by Jim Lahey of the Sullivan Street Bakery, this is bread that sort of makes itself. I ran across the street, bought some Fleischmann's yeast, and followed the directions for mixing it with water, salt, and flour. I left the dough to rise overnight and, in the morning, put it in the Le Creuset Dutch oven I normally use only for lamb and beef braises, and then into a 450-degree oven.

An hour later, out it came. It was—bread! It wasn't *good* bread—it didn't have many of those nice, irregular bread bubbles, and I must have put in too much yeast. It was oddly bitter. But it was bread, and I can't explain how weird and pleasing this was. It was as if you had put a slosh of stuff in a bowl and it had come out a *car*, with a gleaming front and a good smell inside.

For the next couple of days, I became, for the first time in my life, acutely bread-conscious. *So many breads!* I marveled as I stared at the bread counter at Dean & DeLuca. I thought of the bread I loved to eat. There was the big, round pain Poilâne at the bakery in Paris, sour and stiff and yet yielding to the bite; Montreal bagels, sweet and sesame-rich; and real croissants, feathery and not too buttery. Could you really *make* these things?

"If you're so interested in bread-making, you should apprentice with someone big," said Martha, who had declared herself hors de combat, waiting for her wood. "Someone who yells at you a lot and teaches you what's what. You know. Apprentice to a baker. Every writer does that now."

I wouldn't want to learn just one thing, though, I mused. "It would have to be someone who had range, so I could learn how to bake pain Poilâne and Montreal bagels and croissants, and—"

I stopped in midsentence. The larger implication of what I had been saying hit us both. We looked at each other balefully, as those on whom the implacable hand of fate has fallen.

"I'll call her," I said.

When I got my mother on the phone a few hours later—you often have to leave a message, because she and my father are always out in their fields, building things—she was delighted at the idea of a bread-baking-master-class weekend. "Yes, yes, dear," she said. "It's so funny you called. I'm just working on a new series of water-buffalo-milk ice creams. You'd love trying them. Do come for a visit as soon as you can. I'll show you how to bake anything in the world you like."

———

A WEEK LATER, I found myself once again in the backseat of my parents' all-purpose child-mover and SUV. My parents live these days on a farm in what their six children think of as remote rural Ontario—a designation my parents emphatically reject, pointing out that it is only a three-hour drive from the Toronto airport, not seeing that a three-hour drive from the Toronto airport is *exactly* what their six children mean by "remote rural Ontario." They retired a decade ago to these rather Berkshire-like hills, after a lifetime as college professors. Now my father continues behind the wheel, always ready to drive—sometimes out in search of exotic woods for my mother to use in her furniture making, sometimes, incredibly, for twelve or fourteen hour trips to see a grandchild or glimpse a new great-grandchild. (They have fourteen of the first kind, and, at last count, seven of the second.) My mother continues to bake, though the rolled-out strudel that is the first evidence I remember of the power of skill to make beauty, or at least something delicious, has vanished from her repertoire, replaced, as I had learned already as a boy, with other, more French *delices*.

The vibe of their property, one of their kids has pointed out, is somewhere between *A Midsummer Night's Dream* and *The Island of Dr. Moreau*. Bosky though their woods are, within them are a host of strange new buildings that my mother has designed and she and my father built, laboriously, with local lumber, responding to their own unaltered eccentricities and the changing passions of their grandchildren. There is a Japanese teahouse, complete with a little Hiroshige-style arched bridge; an Elizabethan theater, with a thrust stage and a "dressing house" above; a garden-size chess board with life-size pieces, made when my own son was in the midst of a chess mania, now long past; a Tempietto, modeled on Bramante's High Renaissance design; and a Pantheon, a domed building lined with niches, in which sit portraits, with quotations, of my mother's heroes—Galileo, Shakespeare, Darwin, Emily Dickinson, and Bach among them.

My parents, you might gather, are unusual people, although, to be honest, "unusual" is not really an unusual enough word to describe my mother. One of the first women in North America to earn a PhD in mathematical logic, she became a notable linguist and (as she would be the first to tell you) also reared six kids, for whom she cooked a big French-ish dinner every night. We have a complex relationship. I know that I am more like her than I am like anyone else on Earth, for good and ill. Like her, I cook every night. Like her, I offer hyperemotional editorials directly at the television at moments of public outrage, to my children's embarrassment. Like her, I look accusingly at my children when they fail to devour some dish that, backed into a corner, they had acceded to at seven in the morning. ("What do you want tonight, salmon or capon?" "Uh, whatever. Salmon.")

I even inherited some minute portion of her creative energy, which once launched a thousand shapes—from doll houses to linguistic theory—so that, coming home after an eight-hour family trip (during which I, like her, will have, until recently, left all the driving to my spouse), I can actually enjoy whipping together a big meal, with a hot dessert, for the gang. I once realized, with a sense of fatality, that I have written long essays in praise of nearly every hero in her pantheon up there on the Ontario hill—only Bach and Emily Dickinson had escaped my attention, or her gravitational pull.

Into one of her areas of particular mastery I didn't even try to follow her: baking bread. As a kid, I never left for school without being equipped with croissants or pain au chocolat or cinnamon babka or sticky buns, often in combination; on the morning before a big holiday, the kitchen always looked like a Left Bank bakery.

As we pulled up onto the property, my mother turned around. "Did you see our new building, dear?" she asked.

"Sure," I said. "Last visit I saw it." I thought she meant the Pantheon, or maybe the Tempietto.

"Oh, no, not *that*," she said, as though a Pantheon were as commonplace as a lawnmower shed. "I mean our Érechthéion!"

Alarmed by the name, I peered out the left-hand window, and, insanely enough, there it was: in wood and plaster, a nearly full-scale model of the Porch of the Caryatids from the Acropolis, with its six Ionic columns and six draped female figures supporting the roof. The Greek girls were about six feet tall, and, in the Ontario farmland, they looked pretty impressive, though something about the way the figures were incised gave them a demure Canadian quality.

"It's beautiful, Mom," I said feebly.

That night, we sat down to a dinner mostly of breads—sketches of the weekend to come. I recognized most of them from childhood, but there was a dinner roll that was the best dinner roll I had ever eaten: flaky and rich and yet somehow reassuringly simple and eggy.

"Oh, that's my *broissant*," she explained gaily. "It's my own invention. It's brioche dough given a croissant treatment—egg dough with butter folded in in layers. Do you want to try it? We'll do it tomorrow."

My stomach filled with gluten, I took the books on bread baking and bread history I had brought with me and went back to my old bed.

———

AT THIS POINT, I should pause and insert lots of stuff about ancient yeasts, the earliest known instances of bread, bread-in-Sumer-and-Egypt lore, and then a joke or two about the Jewish invention, on the lam, of the unleavened kind. Yeast as the little bug that changed the world. I will spare the reader this, even if it costs me a few other, less knowing readers . . . for the simple reason that, turning the pages in the bread books, I decided that the worst of modern food bores is the bread bore. Unlike, say, the history of magic, defined by crazily detailed micro-arguments over the source of every card move and the originality of every illusion, the very universality of bread, the simple alchemy that makes it miraculous, can also make it dull to discuss.

But, as I was reminded the next morning—with my mother wearing her flour-resistant "Monaghan Lumber" T-shirt—bread, though perhaps unrewarding as an analytic subject, is fascinating as a practice. It is probably the case that these two things often vary inversely: activities that are interesting to read about (science experiments) are probably dull to do, while activities that are dull to read about (riding a bike) are interesting when you attempt them. What makes something interesting to read about is its narrative grip, and stories are, of necessity, exercises in compressing time. What makes something interesting to do is that—through repetition, coordination, perseverance—it *stretches* time. Stories shorten time, abbreviate the pauses, offer the telling highlights.

In Tolstoy, a Petersburg dinner party that must have taken hours to experience takes minutes to read. But the experience of mastery lengthens time: by making each step fully self-conscious, we live within the moment as we otherwise rarely do. The attempt to banish distraction, which we try and fail to achieve in meditation, for instance, happens unbidden in kneading dough or practicing scales or making tilts in time. Our interiority is stretched like silly putty. We become hummingbirds with heartbeats that, however rapid, can only be experienced by the bird as the natural flow of life, neither fast nor slow, just normal to the task at hand, or beak.

My mother has always been an expert in-depth explainer, although her children have been known to run for doors and leap out windows when she starts to say, "Well, studies show that . . ." I have a fond summertime memory of her explaining Gödel's proof to me; I wish I had retained it, though I recall an indecently vivid picture of sets struggling, in vain, to contain themselves.

Yeast, my mother explained now, is really just a bunch of bugs rooming together, like Oberlin grads in Brooklyn—eukaryotic organisms of the fungus kingdom, kin of mushrooms. "When you mix the little bugs with a carbohydrate—wet wheat is a good one—they begin to eat up all the oxygen in it, and then they pass gas made up of ethyl alcohol and carbon dioxide." The alcohol they pass is what makes spirits. The carbon dioxide is what makes bread. The gas they pass causes the dough to rise. It's what puts the bubbles in the bread. If you bake it, you trap or fix the bubbles inside.

As we mixed and kneaded, the comforting sounds of my childhood reasserted themselves: the steady hum of the powerful electric mixer my mother uses, the dough hook humming and coughing as it turned, and, in harmony with it, the sound of the

Canadian Broadcasting Corporation in the background, offering its perpetual mixture of grave-sounding news and bright-sounding Baroque music. (A certain kind of Canadian keeps the CBC on from early morning to bedtime, indiscriminately.)

Like most good cooks, my mother is sweet-tempered in the run-up to cooking, short-tempered in the actual event. (Her quick, sharp "Gop!," instructing my father to do something instantly, is as familiar to her children as birdsong.) For all its universality, bread's chemistry, or, really, biology, is a little creepy. "The longer it takes the little bugs to eat up the oxygen, the better the bread tastes," she went on. "The high heat of the baker's oven simply kills off the remaining little bugs, while leaving their work preserved in place. It's all those carbon-dioxide bubbles which become fixed as the nice spongy holes in the crumb of the bread." The tasty bits of your morning toast, I realized, are all the tombs of tiny dead creatures—the Ozymandias phenomenon on a miniature scale. Look on my works, you mighty, and eat them with apricot jam.

We turned to the pain Poilâne, whose starter she had made earlier; it now luxuriated under a plastic bag in the sink. You can mix up water and wheat, she explained, put it out in the air, and wait for all the wild yeast that's drifting around in the schmutz of the kitchen to land on it and start eating the carbohydrates. This yeast tends to have more character than the yeast that you buy in the store, because, as every dog knows, the schmutz on the kitchen floor has more flavor than anything else. Well-kept schmutz of this sort provides the sour taste in sourdough bread. (San Francisco has a distinctively sour kind of schmutz, so distinctive that it has a scientific name: *Lactobacillus sanfranciscensis.*) The long-cherished deposit of ancient schmutz—a spongy mess that you can use day after day and even decade after decade, and whose exigencies you, as a baker, basically can't escape—is called, no kidding, "the mother."

"Bread is very forgiving," my mother said, as she turned over the pain Poilâne dough. "In the books, they fuss endlessly, and, you know, I used to worry and weigh, but now I know the bread will forgive. The secret of bread is that bread is much more forgiving than non-bakers know."

We took out the breads that we had prepared the night before. "The broissant is essentially a brioche egg dough with butter folded into it," my mother said. "Now, the trick, dear, about laminating butter is to get the thickness of the butter *exactly* the same as the thickness of the dough." We cautiously beat down the butter into layers. "Then you fold it over in exact thirds, like *this*." She showed me.

We began to fold. And fold. And fold again. As I tried to fold, she frowned ferociously. "You have to even it out so that you don't have those bulges at the corners," she said. The CBC rose in the background. As luck and life would have it, a mildly alarmed Canadian-style piece about gluten allergies and gluten-free diets was on. In a slightly prim tone—as my sister Hilary points out, Toronto is the last big town where "hygienic," a holy word, is pronounced as though it had five syllables—it told of how many people had given themselves a diagnosis of celiac disease, and how our bread-addicted society might be ending.

"That is so stupid," my mother bristled. She went on to rattle off facts about the incidence of celiac disease and the follies of self-diagnosis. But beneath it, I knew, was the simple love of bread. I imagined my mother and myself as the last bread-heads, the final gluten addicts, sitting in a stifling, overheated basement room somewhere, stuffing ourselves with broissants.

We spent two days mixing water and yeast and different

flours, and then we waited for different lengths of time. We did the pain Poilâne, dark and crusty and dependent on a long, long resting period; we did bagels—real bagels, as produced in the Montreal bakeries, with a large hole, a bright sesame glow, and a sweet, firm bite. These had to be rolled, and my mom was impatient with my rolling, since unless you do them just right they bounce back yeastily to their original form.

I was taken by the plasticity of every sort of dough, its way of being pliable to your touch and then springy—first merging into your hands and then stretching and resisting, oddly alive, as though it had a mind of its own, the collective intelligence of all those little bugs. Bread dough isn't like dinner food, which usually rests inert under the knife and waits for you to do something to it: bread dough sits there, respiring and rising, thinking things over.

Then, there are the smells. There's the beery, yeast-release aroma that spreads around the kitchen, the slowly exuding I'm-on-my-way smell of the rising loaf, and the intensifying fresh-bread smell that comes from the oven as it bakes. The deepest sensual pleasure of bread occurs not when tasting but when slicing, cutting into softness that has suddenly gained structure: the pile of yeasty dough, after its time in the hot oven, turned into a little house with a crisp, solid roof and a yielding interior of inner space. Bread is best seen in cross-section, and each cross-section is different. Each bread has a beautifully different weight and crumb as the knife cuts into it. The pain Poilâne style almost squeaks as you cut into it, the sourdough, or levain, that gives it that nice acid bite seeming to protest under the knife; the bagel's firmer flesh is made less resistant by that hole; the broissants crumble, with a spray of soft crumbs, under the lightest touch, the many layers you fold into the puff pastry turning into a house of a hundred floors under your command. And greed can some-times lead you to tear off the end of the softer breads, in a gesture satisfying in itself, even before you bite. (And if all this sounds a touch Freudian for a man baking with his mother, well, the Oedipal dramas we enter knowingly leave us better sighted, not blind.)

As one project followed another, I realized why I had not been drawn to bread baking in the first place. Stovetop cooking is, at a first approximation, peeling and chopping onions and then cry-ing; baking is mixing yeast and water with flour and then *waiting*. The difference between being a baker and being a cook is whether you find waiting or crying more objectionable. Wait-ing is anathema to me, and activity is essential to my nature—a nature I share with my mother. But then it occurred to me that my mom is that anomalous creature: not only a master baker but an *impatient* baker. She fills the gaps created by enforced waiting by being active, so that each bread, as we put it down to wait for it to rise, was succeeded by another bread in need of mixing or punching or rolling. The kitchen of my childhood had filled up with bread as she waited for the rest of the bread to be ready.

———

ON MONDAY MORNING, I packed the loaves and broissants and bagels in my overnight bag. I would take them home to study and share with my own children. I gave my mother a hug. "It's such fun to bake with you, dear," she said. "Of course, I spent years making you bread every morning. We always had crois-sants and muffins and—oh, dear, I *always* had so many things out for you."

Was there, after all these years, a just discernible note of exasperation, a regretful sense that her children's appetites were not equal to their bafflement at her avidity? I realized that I had never once thanked her for all that bread. On the long drive to the airport and the short flight to LaGuardia, with all her bread in my bag, I reflected that the thank-yous we do say to our parents, like the ones I hear from my own kids now—our over-cheery "Great to see you" and "We'll catch you in October"; our evasive "Christmas would be great! Let's see how the kids are set up"—are never remotely sufficient, yet we feel constrained against saying more. (We end phone conversations by saying "Love you!" to our parents; somehow, adding the "I" seems too . . . schmutzy, too filled with wild yeast from the hidden corners of life, likely to rise and grow unpredictably.) We imagine that our existence is thank-you enough.

Children always reinterpret their parents' sense of obligation as compulsion. It's not *They did it for me* but *They did it because they wanted to.* She wanted to bake that bread; you told those bedtime stories every night, really, for yourself. There'd be no surviving without that move, the debt guilt would be too great to shoulder. In order to supply the unique amount of care that children demand, we have to enter into a contract in amnesia where neither side is entirely honest about the costs. If we ever totted up the debt, we would be unable to bear it. Parents who insist on registering the asymmetry accurately (the Jewish mother in a Roth novel, the Japanese father in an Ozu film) become objects of frantic mockery or, at best, pity for their compulsiveness. "All I do is give and give and what reward do I get? You never call!" the Jewish mother moans in the novel, and we laugh and laugh, and she is right—she *did* give and give, and we *don't* call. She is wrong only to say it out loud. In the market of emotions, that sacrifice is already known, and discounted for, as the price of life.

When I got back to New York, Martha was at last ready to make her bread. She had found the right kind of earthenware bowl and the right kind of wooden board and even the right kind of counter scraper. After my weekend with my mother, I offered to show her how to use the dough hook on the Sunbeam, but she looked at me darkly. "My kind of bread isn't made in an electric mixer," she said.

"There's a certain aesthetic to baking my bread," she went on. "Everything has to be clean and nice." She had, I noted, put on a black leotard and tights for the occasion, so that she looked like a Jules Feiffer heroine. She mixed together all the good natural ingredients—the brown flour and the millet and the organic honey—and then laid a length of white linen over the earthenware bowl. "It's not a sweet bread, but it has sweetness in it," she explained.

At last, in the silent kitchen, the dough had risen, and we all gathered around to watch. Her kneading startled her family. She kneaded in a domestic fervor, a cross between Betty Crocker and a bacchante. There was no humming mixer, just a woman and her dough. Then she began to braid three long rolls of dough together, expertly.

"Mom, this is, like, such a *big* bread," my daughter, Olivia, said. "It's like bread you would bring to Jesus."

It was too. And suddenly, crystal through the years, I saw Martha at nineteen, on one of those bitter, beautiful Canadian mornings, eyes turned almond by the cold, fur hat on and high collar up, carrying...a braided loaf, in a basket, tied with a shiny purple ribbon. She *had* baked bread, this very bread, and brought it to me too. And it had been lost in the family kitchen, surrounded by too many croissants and sticky buns and too many chattering and devouring mouths.

She was a baker. We have an urge to make mastery too singular. We assign one person to it and deprecate or even dismiss the possibility of someone else being just as good. It is, so to speak, the curse of the Turk. There are many masters, too often invisible. This had been a kind of curse in my own family, with each of six children announced to have a skill at an early age—Alison's for argument, mine for eloquence, Morgan for drawing, and all the way down to Melissa's for empathy. That these "gifts" might have been real enough does not change the truth that they were also widely distributed, and that assigning each to one was a way of keeping all from everything. We are all more varied and capable than we are often allowed to seem. My wife, whom I thought of as a loaf, was a baker; my mother, whom I thought of as a baker, was a loaf. Our misperceptions of mastery can be as multiple as our grasp of it.

"You brought a loaf like this over to my house!" I said to Martha now. "I see it now. But I can't remember how it tasted." It was an anti-Proustian Proustian moment: memory flooded back in the presence of something that I had forgotten to eat.

"Of course not," she said. "No one noticed. It was just, 'Oh, how nice! Put it there.' I don't think you even ate any. Your mother's whole French thing was so different. It overwhelmed my loaf. I think it was the last time I made my bread."

When it was baked, sixty minutes in a slow oven, her loaf looked beautiful, braided like the blond hair of a Swedish child. The next day, I buttered a slice of it, delicious and long-deferred toast, and had it with my coffee. As toast always will, it seemed morning-bright, and clean of complications. Women, I thought, remember everything. Bread forgives us all.

The Fourth Mystery
of Mastery

The Mystery of Meaning

I SHARED A STAGE ONCE, DURING A MOTH STORY-
telling show, with a distinguished sound engineer named John
Elder Robison. He spoke of his long career recording heavy-
metal music and his work as an electronic instrument-maker—
even making fireworks-shooting guitars for the likes of KISS
and Judas Priest. It was a remarkable life of musical mathematics
and modeling, in every sense.

And then he explained that through it all, he had experienced
an emotional detachment from music, sensing it essentially as
an exercise in engineering. Only in later life, he said, did he get
"diagnosed" as somewhere on the spectrum, and, after treatment, with transcranial magnetic stimulation, for the first time in
his life felt the full force of the meaning, the emotional power, of
music. "I get in my car to drive home, I put on this recording of
Tavares"—an R&B band from the '70s, famous for the *Saturday
Night Fever* song "More Than a Woman"—"and it was like I was
back in 1977 again . . . it was so real . . . all the years I engineered
rock 'n' roll, and people told me I did such a great job of deliver-
ing beautiful music . . . and I could never *feel* it." That night, he
could "feel it, that these were love songs, that they were stories

written for real people." He said, "I could feel it for the first time. I got home, and it made me cry—it didn't make me sad, it didn't make me happy. It just was overwhelming." ("That's some powerful mojo you have in that machine," he said to the "mad scientists" who had pulsed his brain.)

Of all the mysteries that the pursuit of mastery makes us confront, this may be the most amazing: that we can first take sound and turn it into music, and then take music and turn it into meaning. In a sense, this mystery stands in for all the other larger mysteries of meaning—of why the real work when we do it isn't just entertaining or impressive, why we aren't just "taken" by the card trick or a life drawing but moved, engaged, even often impelled by it to dance and cry and map our lives upon it. The last thing we feel about good art is cool. We are so accustomed to this mystery that the fact that it *is* a mystery may surprise us.

It is in music that the mystery of meaning comes closest to our heads and faces: we take mathematical sequences by which air has been disturbed and made to vibrate, by plucking on a string or blowing on a column, and around those sequences we wrap our emotional lives. We don't hear "music." We make and hear love songs, wedding marches, funeral hymns, national anthems—we hum the "Ode to Joy" and wonder if the "Monster Mash" is the name of the song or the name of the mash. We're so good at doing it that it seems no longer puzzling. The rest of the double leaps the mind makes, after all, look almost easy by comparison: we like pictures of babies on their mother's laps in sunlight because, after all, in the world we like sunny days and chubby babies. The stories we tell in literature are most often like the lies we tell in life. But music is simply a set of physical vibrations that reach our eardrums; from those vibrations we make the emotional map of our lives.

I feel this so deeply since, of all the urges for meaning and learning that I have experienced in my own life, the urge to make music is by far the most powerful I've ever felt. From the time I formed Beatles chords on a guitar at twelve till today, when I struggle through "Lullaby of Birdland" on piano— George Shearing's widow lives in our building and has generously invited me up to their apartment to play on the late, blind pianist's piano after I learn it—music is the thing I love most in the world. I am, as I said to Robison backstage at the time, sort of him in reverse—not someone highly skilled in music who can't get its meanings but someone so overwhelmed by the meanings of music as to make him look past the fact that he has no particular skill at it. I came to New York intending to be a songwriter and now find myself in late middle age employed as a lyricist and librettist, with joy and some skill and facility. You can't have spent your life weighing words for a living without having a knack for making words fit syllables and stresses; my songs are, I'm sure, the best thing I've done—a feeling shared by every songwriter, amateur, professional, or master.

———

BUT HOW DOES the meaning of music happen? How does air make music, and then the mind make meaning? And how then does the search for musical meaning make masters of its own? As usual, a little science, a little sociology, and then a little sense, may help.

There are people who study the meanings of music scientifically, and they have made real discoveries. There seem to be, for instance, two "systems" in the brain that respond to music. One is "veridical" and responds to the pleasant sounds of the songs we already know. The other is "sequential": it anticipates the next note or harmonic move in an unfamiliar phrase of music and is stimulated when the music follows the logic of the notes or surprises us in some way that isn't merely arbitrary. We recall the meaning of single harmonies from the melodic sentences they conclude. We "learn" music as we learn language, and, with both, our mind disguises from us the complexity of our brain's calculations. The poignant C-major seventh saves your life when your emotions are already pitched somewhere around a hard-edged, unresolved G7.

On the other hand, and in other ways, music seems to lie well *outside* the normal workings of the mind interpreting its environment. Melody, and for that matter most Western counterpoint, is based on steady tones—and steady tones are almost nonexistent in nature. The natural environment doesn't have periodic pitch: Leaves, winds, and rain don't have a harmonic structure. Cognitive psychologist and music student Albert S. Bregman has made a daring suggestion: that music is essentially a form of what he had dubbed "chimerical perception." (The Chimera was a composite beast in Greek mythology with the head of a lion, the body of a goat, and the tail of a serpent.) Bregman gives as an example of an auditory chimera, "a heard sentence that was created by the accidental composition of the voices of two persons who just happened to be speaking at the same time."

Natural hearing, he explains, tries hard to avoid chimeric percepts—we don't *want* to hear a composite voice, and our brains work hard to separate them when we listen to a conversation—but it is the special role of music to try to create those perceptions, to populate our mental universe with chimeras. We put together and "accept the simultaneous roll of the drum, clash of the cymbal, and brief pulse of noise from the woodwinds as a single coherent event with its own striking emergent properties."

Our auditory-processing system intends to eliminate auditory chimeras—but music is an auditory chimera on the rampage. Music asks us to stop and hear both the snake as it slithers and the vines rattling that it slithers on and take pleasure in its double nature because we know that we are safe.

Daniel Levitin, another well known "psycho-acoustician" and a practicing musician, too, studies the nature of expression in music. Using a Yamaha Disklavier that can record the precise fingering and pressure of a pianist, and then play it back, Levitin and his team at McGill University in Montreal had a professional pianist play Chopin into it, and then laboriously spoon-fed the expressive dimensions, the "phrasings," into a computer program, registering how hard he pressed down on the keys, and then how much he varied speeds within a fixed rhythm. Then they taught the computer to intensify or minimize those variables—to play versions of the same Chopin piece with much more variation within the tempo, or much less, with more variations within the volume of notes, or much less.

It turned out, not surprisingly, that people sought out an optimal middle of expressiveness; they liked the Chopin the way the pianist had played it, with enough rubato and musical italicizing to indicate the presence of a particular player, but not so much that it all became randomized mush. That shouldn't really be surprising. We prefer a touch of vibrato in a singer's voice to the full Kate Smith tremolo. We like a pianist who, as the phrase so rightly has it, tickles the keys, and dislike one who bangs them. Psychoacoustics matters: it charts with a new precision the hazy but crucial area between what the sound-sensitive ear hears and what the pattern-detecting mind infers, which is exactly the place where music happens.

The truth of music resonates with that central truth of magic.

The "Too-Perfect" theory beloved of the sleight-of-hand man plays a role in Mozart too. We need evident imperfection in order to be perfectly impressed. All the expressive dimensions whose force in music Levitin had measured and made mechanical were defections from precision. Vibrato is a way of not quite landing directly on the note; rubato is not quite keeping perfectly to the beat. Expressiveness is error. What really moves us in music is the vital sign of a human hand, in all its unsteady and broken grace. Ella singing Gershwin matters because Ella knows when to make the words warble, and Ellis Larkins knows when to make the keyboard sigh. The art is the perfected imperfection.

———

INDEED, THIS TRUTH of mastery occurs again and again. Art is our word for a beautifully blurred signal. The most obvious and straightforward examples are in the eloquence of the eraser, opening up the signal so that we can project form into it. The blur and grisaille of the sketch, or the same in Chinese ink painting, are invitations to broaden our response, not narrow it. The "beholder's share" expands as the blurred paint extends. Arturo's hand, directed at the other driver, meaning both bless you and fuck you, was in a way the primary aesthetic gesture: ambiguous by nature, it went wherever you wanted it to go.

But this simple, almost crude physical trick of mastery—which, followed to its own logical end, would make all pictures one blur, all music one quaver—points to a larger horizon of feeling. We find meaning in one thing by enlarging the area of reference, making it not more precise but less, by a horizontal leap relating it to something larger. Meanings expand as our contexts expand. Art only becomes articulate within a history, each splashy "me" of Pollock's pouring becoming a cool "you" of Warhol's appropriation; and the more of the history one knows, the more specific our response can become, each picture taking meaning only from the one that came before. Music, too, becomes mood over time, gathering us in its voyage—traveling from minor to major, reminding us of how blue notes break expectations and diminished fifths suggest hard edges.

In this way, the perceptual psychology of music offers a series of dimensions, of techniques—the power of expressive imperfection, the force of chimerical perception—that may help open the puzzle of musical meaning. For those dimensions on their own would be merely mechanical. And on inspection, we realize that John Elder Robison wasn't missing some mechanism in his mind that, flipped on, allowed him suddenly to find music meaningful in a way that agrees with the rest of us. It wasn't some specific encoded emotion but the existence of *connections* between emotions, which most of us find easily, that he was missing. When he heard Tavares on that car trip, what he heard, he explained, was 1977—he could smell the cigarettes in the room where he heard the band. The emotion, often undefined, within the music, flooded over it. Read Robison's excellent memoir, *Look Me in the Eye*, and one learns that the "bombardment" of his brain by the magic box came relatively late in a process of self-discovery already begun. He was struggling to connect, to learn, to recognize his own "spectrum" state. Laboriously, sometimes by rote and sometimes by sheer intuitive connection, his "neural plasticity" had already been expanded, making it possible for him to play a deeper role as a husband and father, make more and more varied friends, engage in many other dimensions of human interchange.

He hadn't gotten "better" by "narrowing in" on the signal, hadn't gotten in touch with the emotion of music by channeling its message more precisely. He felt the music by broadening the range of his responses so that the vibrations in the air vibrated along with new dimensions of meaning in his mind. Before meaning came to music, one reads in his memoir, he had already allowed music into a wider pool of experience. The Tavares song he heard was less like a theorem and more, well, more like a woman. He heard mid-'70s disco and sexual desire where before he had heard sound in a space. Whatever the particular additional value of electromagnetic pulsing, what it opened up for him was not a neat channel, like a key in a lock, but a heightened sensitivity to many new dimensions of meaning, a sudden understanding of a larger game that other people were playing that until then he had missed.

Music doesn't carry meaning the way that an encoded message does. It carries meaning as a walk in Venice does, through the shock of novelty, the effects of surprise, the fascination of glimmer on the water, the improbability of architecture so near to being dissolved by its own reflection. When we hear Mozart's slow movement to the A-minor piano concerto, it, too, is more like watching waves or flames in a fireplace than opening a letter. Intentionally crafted though its elements are, it produces feelings not of being told a truth but of being swept away by a musical revelation.

———

ONE MEANS OF anchoring music is through the words we attach to it. This runs the range from religious chants—the earliest statement of the Christian creed is in sung hymns—to the ordinary material of popular song. This is the part of musical work in which I have direct and compound experience. I have been allowed to have many masterly musicians—and, in David Shire, one great master of melody—as colleagues and collaborators and occasional sparring partners, and what I have found in their company is anything but mechanical, some mix of head and heart and competitive energy and sheer youthful brio, even into their eighties, that astonishes me with its composite craft. It is not entirely by accident that the songwriters in the musical theatre are always called "the boys" or "the girls" even when their composite age adds up into three figures, just as it is not crazy that the dancers are always called "the kids" even when they are pushing fifty. Their occupations draw on still-adolescent energies, on the sense, tied perhaps to memories of first sexual experiment, that though this thing has been done before, we can still do it better.

During the past decade, I wrote an oratorio with the inspired composer Nico Muhly. The story we told was that of the great computer scientist Alan Turing, and it was sung by the countertenor Iestyn Davies. I was working on the libretto for the song cycle even as I was also writing the script, which is oddly called "the book," and the words, which are less oddly called the lyrics, to a Broadway-style show.

In the commercial theatre, every syllable, no exaggeration, gets argued over: does it lead with the inevitable pull of emotional logic to the next step in the story? In our Barbican-directed oratorio, though, a great deal of indirection and obliquity was welcome. If the concert audience is baffled, they are intrigued, even impressed. In show business, if they are baffled, they leave. In our age, the difference between entertainment and art is that in entertainment we expect to do all the work for the audience, while in art we expect the audience to do all the work for us.

But the deeper relation between words and music—how they land in the listener's ear, and then her soul—is more complicated than it seems. Music and words together, no matter how hard we craft them for lucidity and shape and dramatic clarity, exist in the end in an older realm of magic and enchantment, a place where the nursery rhyme and the church hymn and the pop single all meet. They work as spells do—that is, either entirely, or not at all. We sing—and the magic door swings open, or it doesn't, and there's no explaining it. Three boys from Liverpool sing, "*Yeah, yeah, yeah,*" and the world turns off its axis. Had they sung, as Paul McCartney's father wanted, "yes, yes, yes," the old path would not have changed.

The libretto writer is not merely the junior partner. The libretto writer is not *even* a partner, more like the man who sweeps out the candy wrappers from the theater floor after the patrons leave. Who now remembers the name of the man who set the texts for Handel's *Messiah*? The only libretto writer whose name anyone remembers—other than the great lyricists of the American musical theatre, the sacred law firm of Mercer, Loesser & Hart—is Lorenzo Da Ponte, who is my hero. He was Jewish and a priest, a Venetian, and a New Yorker. It's a sympathetic package. He wrote the three operas that may well be the height of all artistic creation: *The Marriage of Figaro*, *Così Fan Tutte*, and *Don Giovanni*. But still, he wrote for, more than with, Mozart. Flowing through the easy rhyming of Italian, he set a mark with Mozart that would only be equaled a century later by Lorenz Hart, employing the far more angular and rhyme-resistant language of midcentury New York. It is the most pleasing of fearful symmetries that the two greatest rhyming lyricists in theatrical history, though separated by a century, were both Jewish, both addicted to nightlife, both affiliated with Columbia University (Da Ponte taught there, and Hart went there), and one was named Lorenz and the other Lorenzo. Mamas, don't let your babies grow up to be librettists—or if you do, name them Larry. Yet both are rightly seconded to the composers of genius they served. Music heard without lyrics may be less memorable; but lyrics read without music are always disappointing. The sounds remain, but the shapes are gone.

The real challenge in writing words for music lies in the tiny space between convention and contrivance. Musical theatre of all kinds, whether leading to song or aria, from the highest of Mozart to the lowest, or most pop, of One Direction, is inherently conventional, stylized, in its way limited. It has to be. It depends on a completely unreal convention: people singing when they would speak. Rhymes and English oddities shape one's language as much as one's emotions. For the Turing piece I wrote the lyrics first, and tried, as best I could, to capture in stanzas the *sound* of a man caught between great clarity of mind and confusion of the heart: lucid about ideas, muddled, or repressed, about emotion and desire.

––––––

MEANWHILE, THE LONG and distinguished history of that narrower but incredibly rich subsection of musical theatre that we call the Broadway musical—well, it shows that there is nothing like trying to make two hours of amiable, middlebrow entertainment for a large popular audience to create permanent, bitter, undying enmity among the creative people who are doing it. The history of the musical theatre is, as the Broadway producer Jack Viertel once wrote, simply one of Jewish men yelling at each other. Richard Rodgers first resented Hart, then came to despise Hammerstein, while when Rodgers and Stephen Sondheim worked together, they came to hate each other so much that only their mutual hatred of the book writer, Arthur Laurents, allowed them a moment's respite from their quarrels. More simply, everybody always hated Jerome Robbins. The legends are legend: Once the incomparable composer and lyricist Frank Loesser told a director to tell an actor not to sing a song the wrong way, and after the director obligingly did it, Loesser screamed at him anyway, "But you didn't hit the son of a bitch!" The producer Cy Feuer tells of how Carolyn Leigh, the wonderful lyricist, *actually called the cops* on him once in Philadelphia during an out-of-town tryout— actually went outside and got a police officer to arrest him for having cut one of her songs. I am certain that his story is perfectly true, and the only surprise is that the cop didn't get into the spirit of the thing, once inside the theater, and club somebody himself after offering his notes. The director of my own musical says that he will call his memoir *I Didn't Know Grown-Ups Could Talk That Way to Each Other*, after what his frightened eight-year-old daughter remarked once upon seeing a normal rehearsal session for a nascent musical comedy.

Why does musical theatre make men and women miserable? And what part of the mystery of musical meaning might their misery explain? One answer takes us back to the question of identity, the way that the author of a work effects our understanding of its meaning. For exactly what makes musical theatre so perplexing and hard is that there is no "natural" author of a musical.

By natural author I mean the one who takes authority more or less inevitably owing to the nature of the form. The director, for instance, is the natural author of a movie. While there are many producers' movies and more screenwriters' movies than any director likes to admit, the director is the natural source of authority, coaxing out the performances, allowing the improvs, and making the cuts in the editing room. It is the director who, in every sense, calls the shots. Even if you tried to take authority away from him or her, it would be hard. If you started movie-making over from scratch, the guy or girl who played the director's role would still mostly be its author. That's why the French movie critics of *Cahiers du Cinéma* were not wrong to see even the old-studio-system Hollywood movies as the product of authors, or "auteurs," like Howard Hawks and Victor Fleming. A choreographer, in the same way, is the natural author of the dance: they get the credit whether they entirely deserve it or not. A dancer may deserve most of the credit for a dance and the editor, once in a blue moon, most of the credit for a book. No matter: the vast preponderance of times, the natural author is the actual author, and the rare exceptions leave those who feel cheated grumbling, off to the side.

But a musical has no natural author. It has five or six or seven, each of them often a master in his or her own right. The composer is the actual author of the most powerful emotional beats in the piece—we remember Richard Rodgers's music in *Carousel* far more than any other element—but composers tend to be inarticulate and are often out-talked or out-argued by their script-smart fellows in the rehearsal room. The book writer, as they are archaically still called—elsewhere, simply, the playwright—is by far the most important maker, but though they provide the structure in which the songs may take place, no one recalls the structure, only the songs. Some of the best book writers are obscure to the point of anonymity, even though their contribution was the essential one. They live in frustration. The director is often powerful to the point of omnipotence, but no one except special groups of insiders will ever think of it as the director's show. The lyricist, meanwhile, has a reasonable claim to be the actual author of the show—the music's emotional force *only* takes specific meaning through the words it accompanies—but he or she will often end as the most invisible of all. It is not at all unusual for even the most literate of singers to announce "A Burt Bacharach song" instead of a Bacharach/David one. Meanwhile, the choreographer believes himself to be the natural author of all the things the director is doing badly but is also sure that the director will get the credit even if the choreographer fixes it. And while the actors play a crucial role in creating the piece—one bad actor or miscast or merely out-of-tune actor can ruin the work of eight years—actors, as one of the best of them said to me, have always to show passion and accept powerlessness. They know that they have no real authority at all.

And when there is no natural author, there is a natural vacuum, and into that vacuum rush all the resentments of a lifetime. Seven creative people collaborating where each thinks their contribution is key is not possible. A seven-person creative team of equals is called a war.

And yet the real task of the musical theatre remains noble: taming the music. I don't mean taming in the sense of neutering or curbing. I mean it as old-fashioned lion-tamers did, mastering a wild thing by a slow dance of approach and avoidance, allowing it its power while trying to exhibit its force. Music has so *much* emotional force that we can only serve it, channel it, make it mean with maximum intensity.

Why, then, does it go on—and why does it remain the goal of writers who have known success elsewhere to take part in it? That question has a simple explanation. There is nothing in the arts that can equal the feeling of satisfaction when the musical theatre works. When a singer and a song and an emotional moment all strike the audience together, it has a thrill keener and sharper-edged, at once exultant (because they felt it!) and mischievous (because you had been conspiring for months to make them feel so!), than anything else in art.

A single touch of contrivance spoils it all. Anytime we feel the musical's authors creating coincidence or engineering emotion, making melodrama rather than musical drama, we rebel inside. In *Così Fan Tutte* we accept the convention of disguised Albanians. But we accept it because Mozart writes his most sublime music for the silliest parts. If it became cute, we would reject it. That "yeah, yeah, yeah" mattered because it was what such a boy would actually say to a friend about a girl. The smirk, or the hacks' weary, instantly recognizable musical clichés, are both enemies of enchantment, and without enchantment, music and words mean nothing.

The force of music is mysterious. We know this from the experience of the music we love that it casts a spell before it spells out sense. Music is so emotionally overwhelming that it pushes the discursive and explanatory roles of language aside—and it is part of the job of the writer to get out of its way. Even in Handel's *Messiah* we recall lyrical fragments more than whole stanzas. "Unto us a child is born," "how beautiful are the feet," "All we, like sheep." When we think through our experience of our favorite oratorios, our favorite arias, our most important pop songs, they are almost always the experience of a forceful fragment: three or four words—"how beautiful are the feet" or "shake it up, baby."

It is a strange, semi-physical response, in which the audience does do as much work as the artists. It works or it doesn't. Small fragments of sound and sense strike our hearts as shrapnel strikes our skin; they lodge and wound us, independent of the intended trajectory of the shot. The audiences respond or they don't; they are less like a crew of supercilious analysts and more like a magnet set to one pole or another. If the pole is right, they are drawn irresistibly to the sound onstage. If it isn't, no amount of seduction or intelligence can draw them in, any more than a physical magnet can be made to adhere to metal by goodwill or affection.

Sung words belong more fully to the world of ritual and routine, of incantation and mothers' murmurings, than to the fully
lucid and well-lit world of argument and dramatic advance. They
work, or not.

————

IT SEEMS OUR MINDS make meaning out of music by not
making *too* much meaning out of it. As a young philosopher has
written, the heart of the musical experience is "helplessness"—
not helplessness in the face of confusion but helplessness in the
face of a coherence that surpasses our hopes. I have learned as a
librettist to tiptoe to the edge of argument, and then back off to
the limbo-land of implication and indirection. The most memorable lyric of Steven Sondheim is the most offhand—a rueful
farewell, but exactly to whom or exactly why we never know: I
hear the producer or book writer saying, "Send *in* the clowns?
Shouldn't it be call off the clowns!" But in the clowns must come,
for reasons only clowns and composers know.

Honoring the ancient mysteries of the rituals of word and
sound is where the simplest song, and the most advanced modern music, begin. I have not learned, in lyric writing, why music
matters most—but I have learned a great deal about the power of
voices, the limits of language to explain and its power to invoke,
and about the mysterious, unpredictable magnetism that passes
between an audience and art.

Feeling expands only as our attention widens, as we allow
more in. When we want to learn the meanings of an alien music,
we do much better to expand our empathetic sense of where it
came from and how it mingles with the emotions of the people
who listened to it first than we do by penetrating its acoustic
wave pattern. (One understands the ragas of Ravi Shankar far

most profoundly by watching the movies of Satyajit Ray, which first made them famous, where one senses as a whole the play of ancient and modern, the timeless drone of experience, and the treble arpeggio of individual aspiration, village to city and beyond.)

In plain English, John Elder Robison expanded his meanings by broadening his sympathies. He felt more because he knew more. That's the way we all do it. Music has meaning when we give it something to organize, and the thing it organizes best is us. We live within the roaring of chimeras, and we tame them, so to speak, by taking them out for a walk. Music may be made of whole tones, unheard in nature, but life vibrates around it, and the meaning in music, like the music in life, are all the overtones we can't help but hear.

The Fifth Mystery
of Mastery

The Mystery of Late Style, or,
The Sourdough Starter

MY MOTHER, IN THE TIME BETWEEN OUR BAKING together and my writing this, aged and altered—as, for that matter, so did I, down a slope common to all breathing things. And yet her baking stubbornly continued. It seems as if the thing we've mastered is the last thing to leave our hands, after all the rest has fled. So much so that we have, as lovers of art, a whole conception tied to this truth—the idea of "late style." That's a subject perhaps more beloved of what used to be called connoisseurs than of philosophers of aesthetics, who find it frequently fuzzy. Yet it exists. There is a kind of commonality among a certain class of artists whose heartbeats manage to extend to old age. Titian, Matisse, and Michelangelo are perhaps the most famous ones. In each case, some obstacle to dexterity emerges—if no more than the unsurprisingly shaking hands of an old painter, or in Matisse's case, the onset of arthritis—and the artist makes more of the disability rather than attempting to conceal it.

The gift is, exactly, frequently fuzzy. The nondexterity is allowed to register as a positive force—a kind of ultimate, mortality-defying vibrato. Matisse, confronted by his own newly limited fingers, turned to scissors and colored paper to make his art. What emerged, in masterpieces like *The Swimming Pool*, was not a reduced version of what he had made before but a kind of distilled essence of it, eau de vie Matissean, like the apricot liqueurs they make in France, several bushels of apricots boiled down to an essence of apricotism. Titian, too, who lived and painted on into his late eighties, made the free painterliness of his style into its own subject, with the nightmarish *Flaying of Marsyas* creating a still-unequaled tension between the horrific subject—Apollo skinning alive a faun who dared to challenge his musical supremacy—and the flaming, swirling, aerated rhetoric of painterliness with which it's depicted, painterly music to lament one's life by. To which we could add Monet's last water lilies, and for that matter Billie Holiday's last recordings, where the swinging mischief of her matchless records with Lester Young becomes poised, halting, and tragic, a high late style; or Virginia Woolf's very last diary entry, on haddock and sausage, where a lifetime of punctilious pointillism suddenly has a final comic leap: *You see, I can write anything.*

What all these late styles have in common (and one might add Shakespeare's last lyrics in *The Tempest* to the list) is the sense that some element of the artist's younger lyric style—Matisse's love of pure, unshaded color; Titian's celebration of the visible, painterly hand—persists in a more concentrated and extravagantly unapologetic form. High late style involves a defining trait magnified, without being turned into a mannerism. One need only compare Matisse's late style, forced into existence by incapacity, with Renoir's, also pushed into existence by the arthritis from which that great painter suffered, to see the difference. Renoir tries to do the same thing he had always done, those Mexican-looking sunny and dappled nudes, but the inability to sustain the touch gives them the awkwardness and some of the forced emotion of mere kitsch. We feel the repetition of a manner, not the transcendence of a style.

Willem de Kooning is perhaps the artist most caught between. Anyone who saw the first show of "late" de Kooning in 1981 at the Xavier Fourcade Gallery recalls the miraculous revelation of this painter, caught for a long time in a kind of logorrhea of familiar marks, suddenly painting pictures that seemed as vivid and beautifully unreal as Turner's watercolors, and then slipped into more repetitive patterns. It produced a not-entirely-edifying connoisseur's quarrel between those who see a sharp line between the aged but still conscious work of de Kooning, and the work he made while slipping away. And this in turn is meant by the Romantic insistence that the work made without the wholly conscious mind is just as valid, in another register, as the conscious kind, as we are told that those who go off their meds have not a damaged but another kind of valid consciousness. (Indeed, the question has even been quantified, with a handful of scientists insisting that one can see, in the pattern of "fractals" an artist makes, the typical repeated mark of his or her hand, early signs of approaching dementia.)

———

TRUE IN ART, it is true in life as well. My mother's urge to bake, which tied in her case with a varying urge to give, had largely become simply . . . the urge to bake. Any urge to share had become quite secondary. In hard, unsentimental truth, I suspect that's also true of the major aging artists. One of the things that's striking in Matisse or Titian is how self-enclosed their art comes to be. (Beethoven's late quartets, old in biographical chronology if not in absolute age, are perhaps the best instance of that: written in silence, we overhear rather than hear them.) In Monet's case, we peek into his studio in Giverny rather than going to Paris to see his pictures. The obstacle that blindness put in his way, too, becomes a shared secret rather than a public prayer.

The obstacle is not the way. The obstacle is in the *way* of the way. But our stumbling path around the obstacle may in itself be beautiful, because more visibly humane. My mother continued baking and cooking even as she aged, and though some of it was at her usual level, a habit of *habit* crept in and then triumphed. She worked, this woman whose ease in the fine art of strudel-rolling was my very first memory in life of mastery, increasingly intently, increasingly angrily—if one can imagine an enraged croissant or a pain au chocolat baked in fury—increasingly made for its own frightened sake. *I can still do this. I can.* On that much smaller scale, my mother's baking became, as the years went by and our visits became first more infrequent (it was exhausting to go) and then more frequent (they needed more care), baking for the sake of the bagel. The bagel eaters were left outside the circle of dough.

To be young, one recalls while watching the aged, is not to be in a state of ecstasy but merely to be unimpeded, to be in the world without having undue consciousness of your own muscle and bone within it. It's the same thing we experience when we remove a splinter from our foot; what we get is not happiness in a positive sense but a return to not having to think about the prison and the fact of our flesh. We forget our insides and fold ourselves back out. The true condition of youth is the physical ability to forget ourselves. A friend who is still creative in his eighties points out what he calls the "geriatric possessive": people past eighty, he says, are expected to say, "I'm going to take my bath," "I'm going to take my walk." We can counterpoise that to the pediatric possessive: "You're going to take your bath," "It's time for your nap." Only in midlife do we feel secure enough to enumerate actions as existing individually outside our possession of them: "I'm going to take a bath," "I'm going to take a nap." A bath and a nap exist, briefly, outside our possession of them— they're just around for the taking, we suppose, and always will be. Glenda Jackson, when she played Lear on Broadway at the age of eighty-three, caught some of the indomitable egotism of the aged. Watching her onstage, we were asked to recognize not just the anger but also, eventually, the wisdom of age that resides in refusing to extinguish that anger. *Rage, rage, against the dying of the light.* The old, Shakespeare says, can become, or assist us to become, God's spies. Yet the dim light still lets us see. We turn, after all, to the imagery of the old for comfort; we turn to work marked by the frailties of aging for consolation and enlight-enment. Matisse and painted paper find a new world of purity; de Kooning, on the edge of Alzheimer's, lets renewed simplicity break the hand of excessive excellence.

Swift, in *Gulliver's Travels*, invented the race of the Struld-bruggs in order to imagine what eternal life would be like. Eerily, they were given a precise phenotypic marker, a blemish above the left eyebrow, and were given, too, the ill temper associated with age. Promised eternal life, they were cursed with ever-progressing aging, and were the most miserable people alive. What we want—Swift's point—is not eternal life but eternal youth, and that is beyond our grasp, still.

———

NOT LONG AGO, as I was finishing this book, and talking to my parents in a pained, stumbling manner, I began to think about the sourdough starter that my mother had cultivated for all those years. What would become of it when she was no longer there to make it, use it? And then, speaking to a scientist expert in all things yeast, I found out something startling and oddly comforting. Not only does sourdough starter live forever, yeast begetting yeast begetting yeast, like one of those chains of generation in the Bible—but the traces of DNA from bakers' hands long gone remain fertile within the starter. The schmutz is still present generations later. It is the traces that doubtless make the flavor. I recalled asking a gastronome what accounted for the extraordinary and distinct flavor of the smoked brisket at Schwartz's delicatessen in Montreal. "The schmutz in the smoke room," he said bluntly. It was true: once the back room was cleaned out, the savor and brine and intensity of whole peppercorns was gone.

Our mother's fingers stumble as she ages; yet our mother's hands live on. Shakespeare put his trust to immortality variously in marble monuments and rhymes. "What will survive of us is love," another, more famously sour poet told us—a claim hedged, to be sure, by a sequence of "almosts." The truth is simpler. What will survive of us is schmutz. But then, schmutz, being living, however lowly that life may be, it is perhaps a safer guarantee of eternity than all the marble monuments in the world.

Relieving

MORE THAN WE FEAR BEING EVIL, OR EVEN outrageous, what we fear most in life is being embarrassed. It is the great constraint, and the great propellant, of human accomplishment, and of its opposite, human destructiveness. Much of the worst of history is only comprehensible as a tale of embarrassment feared and, at huge lengths, avoided, or trying to be avoided. The opening of the First World War only makes sense—millions of people walking blindly from uneasy peace and prosperity into hell on earth and staying there for five years—because of the mutual fear of public humiliation on the part of its leaders.

So let us rush to descend to a scale incomparably smaller and yet, in its minuscule nature—Ah! as you will shortly see, the language alone sets me up for a limitless, elbow-in-rib set of double entendres . . . here goes. I went into therapy in the midst of writing this book for a condition that had unduly governed and misshapen much of my life. It is called paruresis, and is known, misleadingly, as shy-bladder syndrome—misleadingly because like all phobias and anxieties, however absurd it seems to outsiders, it is pernicious and life-dominating, even at moments life-ruining, for its sufferers. In plain, embarrassing English, I was for fifty years unable to urinate on planes or in public places of any kind, and having, as people will, developed a series of coping mechanisms to deal with it, I found myself the prisoner of the coping mechanisms, and limited in the choices I could make in life. I could get through a six- or seven-hour flight in discomfort but was terrified of trying to go farther. Any long-distance trip, a literary festival in India or Australia, was off-limits. (My family was generally aware of this, as they, of course, struggled with issues of their own.)

How this started or where it came from, I'm not sure. One of the things I learned when I went at last to a curious and gifted therapist to master it is that tracing a phobia or fear to its traumatic source is usually a loser's game, since the "source" more often than not isn't particularly traumatic, and even more often can't be located at all. We're not afraid of flying because we once were in a plane that almost crashed or knew someone who was, or frightened of heights because a friend once nearly fell from a building. The classic traumatic patter of Freudian scare movies of the '40s—the way that Ingrid Bergman figures out that Gregory Peck's terror of white-tine marks on a tablecloth in *Spellbound* traces back to a childhood skiing accident—are now mostly known to be figments, fictions we make up retrospectively. Even the most nastily insidious of the eating disorders that afflict so many young women—though generally assigned to cultural fears and patterns—are rarely traceable to one source or moment.

Yet no one can help but locate his own or her own phobia in some larger orbit of temperament and terrors. It is our way of dignifying our embarrassments. So, it did seem to me that my issue had grown up slowly over time into the wall that it had become. Hypervigilant about other people's attention as I was, the knowledge of the line outside the airplane bathroom had become a lockdown device of its own. In a mood of self-flattery, I ascribed it to the same hyperattentiveness to other people's moods and feelings that made me an observant reporter; in a perhaps more acute mood of self-criticism, I ascribed it to a desire for other people's approval that made me an unsteady advocate of my own causes.

And, lest you, my reader, merely grimace at or mock my discomfort as too trivial for words or worry . . . let me assure you, let me *persuade* you, that shy bladder is not a "shy" disorder. It is a fiendish, dominating, and cruel one. It means that at a play, by intermission the sufferer is in intense need of relief and knows that he can't seek it in the crowded and, to him, smelly men's room of even a dignified West End or Broadway theater. His urgency cohabits and diminishes the pleasure he takes in Patti LuPone's performance. It means that out for dinner he is already thinking of a taxi home to leave it.

Worst of all, it means weeks of anxiety preceding any long-distance airplane trip, followed by hard-breathing anxiety during the trip—which, of course, only increases the panic/"lock up" reaction when he tries, dreading the result, the bathroom. Desperate to urinate, pressing hard to do it, the body absolutely *refusing* to obey, no unlocking possible. (I know that those who do not suffer from paruresis can't/don't believe that this is possible—c'mon, you just pee! for God's sake. But it is.) You do not know, cannot imagine, the extent of the pain and panic it induces.

Insomnia in its more wracking cases—which to be sure I did suffer from once when younger—is the only thing I have to compare it to, and God knows insomniacs suffer. The same absolute refusal of the body to do what bodies are designed to do. We are meant to put our heads down and lose consciousness—millions upon millions of people are doing it right now, this minute! it's the most instinctive and reflexive of human acts—and the insomniac cannot, no matter how tired she may be, no matter how normal sleep is, no matter how natural it might be, fall asleep. The eyes shut, breathing starts, consciousness simply refuses to shut off. It isn't that you "can't sleep," it's that your body *won't* sleep, has set itself against sleep even while making you desperate for it. And then the mounting anxiety that one *won't* sleep, will never sleep again.

But even insomnia, brutal though it is, is at least treatable—if certainly not curable—with pills. Paruresis is not. Xanax won't relax the bladder; Ativan won't release the urethra. The extremity of the discomfort dominates back in one's buckled-in seat, when the only release is hours away. (I have learned the story of a leading American composer, Chester Biscardi, whom my son Luke had studied music with; the author of one of the most beautiful of modern love songs, "At Any Given Moment," and a paruresis sufferer, Biscardi had boarded a plane to go to Berlin to see the premiere of a proud new work—and had had to retreat in panic from the plane and the trip for fear of the tiny washrooms. The condition exacts costs.)

The "coping mechanisms," that is, the "avoidance behaviors," consist chiefly, in my case, of avoiding all liquids for an hour before the flight and then during it and reading intently some book of military history—military history because it is somehow absorbing without being challenging, one floats off into someone else's battle. It's a form of suffering that is extreme while it endures, accompanied by a sense of panic—what if I burst, what if my bladder explodes from overloading? (This can't happen, I'll rush in to assure the reader—to assure myself, panicked by my own sentence—but fears are not based on what can happen but on what one fears *might* happen.)

Yes, yes, yes—by the standards of suffering, physical and mental, this one is still comic, trivial, funny, small. I have, in the past year alone, seen a friend die of ocular cancer—cancer of the eye! God help us, it metastasized to his lung. And I have read at length all about tic douloureux, that most horrific of incurable and unchangeable pains, having written recently about the case of Robert Sherwood, who suffered from it, the playwright who admired and championed unduly early my beloved Buster Keaton. *Those* were pains! *That* was suffering! Those were worries. (I recall my one mild, backwoods brush with that kind of pain, when I briefly had shingles on my facial nerve, and the note of suicidal panic at having to deal with it. Fortunately, marijuana and rum intervened long enough to get me past the weeks' endurance.)

But, and this is a truth that must be said, over and over: suffering is intrinsic to the human condition, and so we cannot grade it on any kind of absolute scale. What we feel is what we feel, and though it may be true that we cry when we have no shoes until we meet a man with no feet, the larger truth is that having no shoes is our only way of beginning to understand what it must *feel* like to have no feet. Deprivation, discomfort, unhappiness—these cannot be wished away by pointing to those who have better reason for them than we do. If we could be cured by the truth that someone is suffering more, then human suffering would long ago have been cured. The Buddha's point, as I understand it, was not that suffering was an illusion but that it was the permanent fact of human existence, one that could only be honored by being universalized. We could see that all suffering is essentially alike, and permanent, and therefore to be understood rather than graded.

It was exactly its universality that made it "ungradeable." The essential point, the point of points, is that we cannot compare sufferings. That is why all the dismissive rhetoric of "first-world problems," as somehow opposed to real ones, is so frustratingly misplaced. Of course we should put our problems in a proper hierarchy of problems, from the most severe to the more trivial. But we cannot help but experience what we experience. The truth of the hummingbirds' heartbeats—that our lived experience is all on one level alike, if our manner of experiencing it is not—is the truth of the shy-bladder sufferer's bladder. Comparing it to another's won't alter it. We live trapped within a self that makes its own dimensions, its own axes, of pleasure and pain. To honor our discomforts at our body's insistence is to honor our selves. A soul is simply the part that lies within the intersecting axes of pleasure and pain and self-knowledge. It sprays out into the world, if we let it.

———

I WAS PAST SIXTY when I finally decided to do something about my peculiar suffering. And so I found a therapist whose sole, or very nearly sole, task in life was, as he put it with typical pungent indelicacy, to help men talk about their dicks all day long. This would be the hardest mastery of all. I had scoured the Internet for someone who did this work and came—or did my suffering wife come upon it?—upon the name: Dan Rocker.

He had, I discovered when I went to see him in his office on the West Side, a shock of white hair superintending a humorous, sweet-tempered face. He worked with a knowing manner that seemed not ill suited but still surprising for a social worker. (I reflexively called him Doctor, though he quickly assured me that his degree was a master's in social work.) Raised in New Jersey, now living a recognizable life in Manhattan with his two kids and a working wife, he had the gravelly, ironic, at times entertainingly cynical tone of the best friend of Charlie Sheen in an '80s movie about ambition. Not the hero, but the hero's wiser office friend, who says things like, "Hey, Charlie. You join the frogmen, you're gonna get your feet wet. C'mon, nothing to resolve a moral crisis like a glass of Patroon."

It turned out, in a way that seemed very much part of the fabric of the New York I had come of age in, that he had made, if not a fortune, then a small reservoir of money as a trader in the market in the '90s. Then 9/11 happened. He was directly across the street from the towers. "I didn't hear the first plane hit, because I was buried in my computer screen, watching the market. And I noticed suddenly that the futures market was crashing . . . turning right down off a cliff. That's weird, I thought. And then I got a message from a friend in Oregon, 'Are you okay?' *That's* weird, I thought. And then I had a call from someone and heard what had happened. My daughter was just a baby, and she was in daycare at Trinity Church, so I rushed over there and then— well, I was actually taking a piss when it happened!—I felt the second plane's strike as a massive vibration between my legs, and I realized immediately what it was. That's another plane. This is an attack."

He lost many after-work friends in the towers, particularly in the decimated brokerage firm of Cantor Fitzgerald, which had (it is still difficult to fully credit this) 658 employees murdered on that day, and decided, more or less quietly, to follow an already-in-place instinct to get out of making money and find something to do that mattered more.

"I had plenty of money and my wife, Rachel, and I decided that it was worth making the break." His first thought had been to have go into hospice work, helping the dying. "But eventually I got rejected for this fellowship I wanted to get! That was a healthy shock to me!"—and then his own severe case of paruresis made him curious about potential treatment for it, and one thing after another had led him to the—really!—International Paruresis Association and to the attempt at last to cure it, to alleviate it. He found himself in the company of other leading paruresis therapists: "I was in psychoanalytic training at the time, and one of them said, we're going to make you into a behaviorist yet!" By behaviorist he didn't mean a therapist who believed, in the classic Skinnerian model, in stimulus and response but rather in what is called cognitive behavioral therapy, or CBT, the belief and practice, very American in origin, that anxiety disorders are best mastered by, as one simple description puts it, "facing one's fears instead of avoiding them. And not looking back, but forwards."

CBT is an interesting and improbable hybrid of behaviorism, with its suspicion of internal thoughts and beliefs, and cognitive psychology, the study of those thoughts and how they affect us. The wisest of the CBT practitioners came to believe that the thoughts *were* the behavior—that if you had somehow argued yourself into the disorder, you could argue yourself out of it again. Briskly against introspection into the mysteries of your mind, it was also briskly in favor of using your mind to break its mysteries.

Winning the argument inside your mind depended on finding the evidence. The evidence would be your capacity to do the thing the anxiety disorder had always told you that you couldn't: sleep or board an airplane or speak to a big crowd or urinate in a public stall. And the way the evidence could be made to win the argument against your convictions was to put yourself in

positions of increasing difficulty. A hierarchy had to be estab-
lished in which you told yourself, and your therapist, what you
couldn't do, and then, having done the easiest thing on the list,
you went on to do the next most difficult. Over time, and not too
much time, the evidence could out-argue the anxiety. You *can* get
on a plane. You will fall asleep. You can pee. (CBT is notoriously
less effective on what still seem to be the deeper disorders—
depression, for instance, or the kind of aberrant behaviors once
called "schizoid"—which seem to have chemical and genetic
bases that defy argument or rational intervention.)

Having hit bottom with his own paruresis—some of the language of twelve-step programs still lingers as rhetorical flour-
ishes within the less pious approach—when, to go visit his
parents in Florida, Dan had booked his *entire family* on a twenty-
five-hour Amtrak train, simply in order to avoid having to use,
or fail to use, an airplane bathroom, Dan had practiced his problem largely away. "I still get locked up, say, ten percent of the
time. But then I go out and practice more and try another bathroom and I see steady progress."

He was reluctant to overcharacterize the compulsions that
drove forward his clients' anxiety; the behaviorist did not spec-
ulate about hidden inner mechanisms in the human mind. But he
did see significant patterns: "Many of my clients work in fields
where hyper-attentiveness is valorized. The very same aspect
of their character that is valorized in their work becomes the
problem in their anxieties. There's a saying on Wall Street, that
if you're going to panic, panic first! So, that panic instinct can
betray you in a bathroom. Some of the traits that make you successful in other aspects of your life make you gun-shy and inhibited in this one.

"I think it's generally true about anxiety. The old example is that of our caveman progenitors—if you're taking in the world and you think that every stick is a snake, when you go take a leak, you'll be unpleasantly worried. But all you have to do is mistake one snake for a stick, and you're finished. So that kind of anxiety, rooted in the flight-or-fight part of our amygdala, is ego-dystonic—it's unpleasant to have this anxiety—but the specificity, attention to detail they demand, are ego-systonic. So, you have to learn that the behavior that benefits you so much in your working life doesn't work for you here."

Paruresis seems to be, not exclusively, but certainly predominantly, a male complaint. Dan guesses that the frequency among his patients, or of those he's treated in group workshops within the International Paruresis Association is, conservatively, something close to ten to one. Women *do* suffer from it, it seems, but some combination of anatomical design, inculcated manners, which makes women more easily sociable in their bathroom habits, or just the truth that the well of anxiety that rises in all of us always find its own fiendish paths to take—eating disorders, it seems, bend, if a little less decisively, in the opposite direction—means that the overwhelming number of patients Dan sees are men. He *has* accompanied women on exposure journeys (that is, bathroom visits) with appropriate cautions and safeguards. ("I'll never be inside a bathroom with a woman," he says.) Conceivably, as always in these things, if there were more women therapists available treating the condition, more women would report it.

————

DAN'S TREATMENT, offered with an appealing mixture of irony, wit, and good humor, and with a sense of shamelessness that shocked me, was to take his patients or clients to public bathrooms in department stores and shopping centers around the city, stay with them or near them as support—working the hair dryer or running the faucets as the occasion dictated—several times a week, and in this way teach them, or their appendages, that they were not in danger in strange bathrooms. "We're learning the difference between difficulty and danger. Or maybe unlearning whatever taught us to identify them" was his theme, the closest that he would come to a maxim or a nameable proposition. You could find urinating in public washrooms difficult, but the sense of panic that the act presented was what you brought to it. There was only difficulty; the danger was your contribution to the porcelain. Discomfort and risk were not the same thing. The line between difficulty and danger, which I had grasped was crucial in learning to drive, had to be turned inside out in disassembling an anxiety. Driving a car was dangerous without being particularly difficult; overcoming an anxiety disorder was difficult without being particularly dangerous. Recognizing the absence of danger was the key to overcoming the anxiety, as much as navigating the presence of danger was the key to driving without panic from Boston to New York.

The answer to drawing, I had learned, was, in a sense, not *to look* but rather to make tilts in time and visualize small African countries, to defeat difficulty with baby steps. The solution to paruresis was peeing. There was a kind of Zen cum American Pragmatism, both Basho and William James, sense to it. There was no "depth" to probe, since the problem was in its nature superficial.

This did not make it easy. But the trick lay in learning to do it, not in learning to do something else that enabled you to do it. There was no trick but the trick. We defeat our fears and phobias not by outwitting them alone but also by out-*dumbing* them, not by outthinking them but by overwhelming them with so much repeated mindless incident that our amygdala just turns off and surrenders, outnumbered.

We break it down and build it back, with the difference that in this case we were tearing down the wall we built to enclose ourselves, made of fears, which now has to be broken down and rebuilt with smaller, simpler blocks of actual experience. In accomplishment, learning to drive or draw or perform a sleight-of-hand card trick, you have to build a behavior, small self-made brick by brick; a phobia was a kind of black-mass parody of accomplishment, a memorial to anti-mastery that, tragically, to the one enclosed within, looks more impressive than the positive kind.

————

FREUD'S THEORY OF CIVILIZATION depends on the idea that primitive men wanted to pee on the fires of other primitive men, and that civilization—art, culture, cooking, building— only began when primitive man zipped up his mammoth-skin loincloth and resisted and went off instead to use the fire to cook and build, setting himself up for shy-bladder syndrome a few millennia further on. Paruresis, on the Freudian view, is the civilizing impulse taken to an extreme case. And this is true to some decent extent: it does seem to unduly afflict those of us, like me, who suffer from an excess of, well, civilization.

That isn't boasting; it's genuinely pained. The bladder sufferer would do anything to be free, to feel free. He can't. Freud thinks—and it may be anthropological hogwash, but it surely captures something profound in our psychology—that we can't pee in part because we are not just reluctant to put out the other guy's fire but are frightened of any fires getting started at all. We are, so to speak, in love with the damp walls and the humid interior of the proto-civilized cave. We cower in fear of the fire.

Is it any wonder we long ago stopped even dreaming of pissing them out?

Absurd though this origin story may sound, it obviously explains something significant that we might also get at through more Darwinian means. It is one of the great jokes of nature—or one of the clearest accidents attendant on, and so proof of, Darwinian design—that in men the urinary tract and the seminal tract focus on a single member. There is no necessity for this, of course, and in a well-designed primate presumably the two functions would have been designed separately. Like the mismatch of babies' brain size and women's pelvic dimensions—which assures that birth will be both painful and, prior to modern medicine, and even with it, alas, hugely dangerous to the mother—the double duty of the penis (and the perineum in women) is a sign of the essentially comic mismatching and mis-making of our bodies. We are jerry-rigged, catch-as-catch-can animals made by chance mutation and competitive sorting, where good enough to reproduce is all the good-enough one needs. Darwinian design is not optimal design; it need only be successful enough to make another animal to work.

So, why does the male member double its function, excretory and reproductive? It seems a horribly inelegant and even inefficient arrangement. High above, the adjacent but not overlapping sensorium of nose and eyes and ears, each with its own province to command, neatly aligned so as to coordinate but each independent in its operation, seems by contrast a prize-winning design of the kind that might have leapt out of some Scandinavian design studio in the 1960s. By comparison, in both sexes the alignment of genitalia has long seemed ill-wrought to the point of being grotesque. In men—at least in men who have, or suffer from, sufficient self-consciousness to be aware of it—the double nature of the organ leads to a double consciousness of its meaning, as though two entirely different organs were at work in each pursuit, one for love and one for riddance.

The answer, according to Jerry Coyne, an evolutionary biologist at the University of Chicago, and author of the best basic explanatory tome on Darwinism, *Why Evolution Is True* is, simply, *Because*. It's the classic adult answer to a child's inquiry: Why do you have to go to bed now? *Because*. Or, Because I said so, the "I" in this case being the forces of evolutionary history that tie us incongruously but inevitably to our fishy past. The answer is . . . *because*. Children rightly object to because as an explanation, finding it almost as bad among explanations as the other parental rejoinder: *We'll see*.

"It's simple," Coyne says. "It's because . . . That's how it started with fish, our ancestors. It's probably too difficult, given the developmental origin of the sperm duct and the urethra to alter—too hard to fix. It's the same reason we have four limbs—because *fish* have four limbs. Maybe we'd be better off with six, like a Hindu god, but it would demand such a huge reengineering of parts that it's simpler to stay with the plan in place So even the question of two tubes is fixed by history. We can't change the big pattern, but we do have secondary fixes . . . there's a flap that closes down the tube, and when one parts shuts off, you can't ejaculate and urinate at the same time. Then you have to open up that duct again. You can fix it secondarily, and that's enough. What would be the advantage of fixing it beyond that? It would take a tremendous rewiring of the urogenital system."

So the answer, as so often with genuine, as opposed to ersatz evolutionary theory, is that there is no good "reason," no "just-so" story that can explain why it had to happen this way or why the way it happened is the best way it could. If the male member were located in the navel and ran on a spigot, paruresis would perhaps not be a "thing." But some other thing would come to take its place as the mind moves to occupy its anatomy and fills the crevices with the anxiety it generates by rote.

But this incongruous doubling not of function alone but of *consciousness* of function is, when one stops to stare at the body, prevalent everywhere. The double functioning of our airway and our food pipe is deathly dangerous in a way that the double functioning of our outward-facing tube is not. The single inhalation pipe is the height of bad design—worse even than the doubled tube. People die from it every day. Yet curiously, this horribly ill-arranged double function seems not to produce anxiety disorders with the same ferocity that the other double functioning does. There *are* people who have anxiety disorders about eating and swallowing—in fact, the two have names: phagophobia, or the fear of swallowing, and pseudodysphagia, the fear of choking. They seem to be fearsome and cruel disorders, not least because they can induce the action one fears, tightening the throat, but are relatively rare—at least, they have no association, like the IPA, single-mindedly devoted to their relief.

The truth is that "because" is not just a good but a profound answer. Because of our history, because of our nature, because it's that way, just because. Freudian therapies depended, to some degree, and were inspired to mimic, what was seen in Freud's time as the scientific shape of explanation, based on a now outmoded form of Darwinian extrapolation. *The true cause of things could be found in the eventful past.* We had evolved as we had for a purpose: having marched forward from our apelike ancestors, we gave up peeing on the fire for housing it inside the hut to smelt weapons with.

The anti-causal cognitive therapy in favor now reflects the anti-teleological biology of our time. There was no primitive trauma in history that made mankind as it is any more than there is a primal trauma in childhood that made us as we are. We are this way because it's the way it happened. Our bodies are shaped so because that was the simplest way to shape them, however badly adapted they may be to many tasks. And similarly, we suffer from these anxieties because we do.

We may be poorly adapted, but we are highly adaptive. The philosopher Ludwig Wittgenstein's pianist brother, Paul, having lost his arm in the Great War, came home and, instead of abandoning music, had a body of new music written for his left hand alone. It is beautiful and virtuosic, and one does not hear, somehow, the empty parts, the missing fingers. Listening, we hear no absences. We actually *know* the sound of one hand clapping; it sounds the same as two.

We are made to be compensatory creatures. Our mechanics do limit our mastery, but they do not cripple our imagination, merely shape it, and the resistance of the body's plan to the body's purposes, though real, is smaller than it may seem. We have such dreams as the stuff we're made of allows, and our little lives sleep well enough within their bounds.

———

I VOWED TO defeat this demon inside me—a demon that was, as Dan emphasized, in many ways *continuous* with myself, angel and demon being my own bifurcation of a seamless self. When the Covid pandemic came and brought the reduction in outside activities of all kinds, I began to concentrate on this therapy, going to Dan as often as three days a week. With the gyms closed, I had taken out my creaky British bike from the basement, a bike we had gotten for the kids back when they were twelve and thirteen, and begun to cycle once or twice right around the park every day.

Dan approved, since, as I had learned, he was a cycling fanatic. He had four bikes of his own—one for the city commute, one for long-distance riding, another two somehow in between—and ruefully referred to himself as one of the legions of MAMIL who filled the park: a middle-aged man in Lycra. He took impossibly long bike rides during the pandemic: up to Riverdale to see his brother, a physician presiding over an emergency pediatric ward; across the George Washington Bridge (on which Dan managed to break a finger on a narrow turn). He thought nothing of taking his bike eight or nine times around the park every morning, where I was hard pressed to manage one, and only rarely two.

But it was a kind of bonding, and he encouraged me to ride my bike right across the park to his office on Amsterdam Avenue. Strangely, his office was in the same building that had been part of my first experience of New York, the Lincoln Towers, where my great-aunt Hannah had lived. Once a cathedral of Upper West Side manners, its small but efficient high-rise apartments companionably filled with secondary singers from the Met and minor faculty from CUNY, a specifically New York Jewish aroma of sponge cake and gefilte fish filling its corridors, with women in "house dresses" cheerfully making the trip to the incinerator drop, it had since become a kind of old people's home, as the formerly spry now aged in place. Their eyes, above their makeshift masks, in that terrible first year, spoke of primal fear and confusion.

Dan's office was on the ground floor. But he believed in confronting the hierarchy directly, and so we would go out together to visit public washrooms, climbing a ladder, in principle, from the clean and less inhabited to the grungy and crowded.

"You brought your bike?" Dan said one day. "Great. Let's go right to the Time Warner Center tower." Dan led me down Broadway, ten or so blocks, weaving in and out of traffic, halting at red lights or, once or twice, looking warily both ways and see-ing no traffic, pushing through against the light. I was startled, alarmed, and hugely, well, relieved, to make it to the door of the Time Warner Center in peace, or at least not in pieces. We locked the bikes, put on our masks, and went bathroom visiting, hierar-chy climbing, defeating the demons by, eventually, if we could, spraying them away. The act of disassembly is as demanding as the act of assembly. We can't outwit our own wits. We can only outwait, and in my case outwater, them.

Dan, I also discovered, had, as a part of his own ongoing treatment, developed a familiarity, a kind of rapturous expertise, with pretty much every public men's room in Manhattan, whose circumstances, limitations, and general standards of cleanliness and character he could reel off with the same offhand authority that he must once have used, in his Wall Street days, for rating Internet start-ups and IPOs.

In fact, when I mentioned that I was riding through Central Park every day, he encouraged me not to be inhibited about try-ing the many men's room there. "Central Park has so many bath-rooms!" he said, almost dreamily. "You are literally *surrounded* by good spots, and there's no place on Earth that's closer to you—that's right there. I've never been on the running track. Maybe that big stone building still has a bathroom in it too? But I'll tell you: Seventy-Second and Hudson River Park: there are nine urinals in a row and seven stalls. Or you can try the one by Tavern on the Green: four urinals, no dividers, though actually one of them's out of order. And three stalls if you get locked up at a urinal. Then there's one by the Delacorte, but the one by the tennis courts is probably close." He brightened. "If you're actually coming up Harlem Hill on the back of the park, right by the Strangers Gate, if you go up to the top of the hill, there's a *beautiful* brick restroom—it's a *classic* one and one: one urinal, one stall." He had, I realized, something of the tone of a real-estate agent running through his listings, even unto the short-hand specialized descriptions.

He was amazingly patient and generous in spirit, washing his hands indefinitely, or else running the hair dryer as he waited. The Time Warner Center became our favorite destination. I had once written a mocking piece in the magazine about the building, ridiculing it as the kind of mall that Manhattan was biologically designed to reject. I now was grateful for its safe-seeming spaciousness (no virus could collect maliciously there) and for its warm, open interior, and above all for its variety of mostly clean and welcoming men's rooms. Just at the moment when malls were becoming redundant and abandoned in the rest of America, the pandemic had made this one invaluable in the city.

"You'll see," Dan said as we went inside, "that there's a good all-purpose six and four on the second floor." Stalls are generally "safer" for paruresis sufferers than urinals, which present a panicky presence for the sufferer. The hierarchy runs from stalls closed and locked, to stalls left unlocked, to stalls with the door left open to the urinal itself, which is the ultimate challenge, in its open condition and frank architectural declaration of plumbing purpose, for any sufferer. The only way around it is to "liquid load"—drink to create a feeling of such urgency that the anxiety is literally washed away. But the paruresis sufferer is so fiendishly skilled at his avoidance strategies, and so grooved in, that he can "shut down" even as he can't. No feeling is more frustrating, or panic inducing, that badly needing to urinate and still being unable to. Dan was utterly non-judgmental of failures and successes, lock ups and liquid loading successes. Practice was neutral, not to be graded or judged, just experienced.

Week after week, we walked the bathrooms of the Time Warner Center, stopping in the Amazon store to look at books and in the Pain Quotidien to get a croissant. We shared stories about our kids; he too had one in an Ivy League school, and we joked about the Ivy League condescending prefatory "So . . ." and about the brutal competitiveness of the admissions policy. Dan was normalizing for me, I realized. We were both hardworking New York dads with baffling, ambitious kids, who shared a peculiar but far from shaming human weakness, an anxiety disorder that we moreover shared with countless millions of others.

The bathrooms were themselves remarkable. Avoiding them as I had for so long, I had never stopped to appreciate how beautiful, how well made, how richly furnished public toilets in Manhattan can be. Pink walls in the terra-cotta style, marble sinks, tile floors as soothingly divided as any in a seventeenth-century Dutch interior—someone had designed all this and made it with a specific and humane eye toward making a necessity of vertebrate life into an elevated social ritual. Dan tried to make me aware, in turn, that, essentially, *anything goes* in a men's room. The anxiety figures we bring to it—the impatient people waiting for you to finish, the imagined man ready to push a reluctant participant aside at the urinal—are our own alone. In truth, you can stand at a urinal for minutes at a time without being dislodged or even much observed, can practically set up housekeeping inside a Time Warner men's room without being noticed.

Well, without being *much* noticed. I did register over time that security guards had been posted near the entrances to the men's rooms at Time Warner, not to discourage visitors but certainly to observe them. Dan was sure that this was being done with an eye toward drug dealers and homeless people who might be using the facilities, but it struck me, upon mordant reflection, that it might have been done in reference to people like us, to the therapists of the world and their clients who would presumably, in their—in our—inexplicable frequentation in constant pairs, have looked dubious of purpose. The use of bathrooms for gay assignations was of course part of the general background noise of the activity. Present from time to time, in the form of polite, implicit solicitation from young men who could only, quite properly, interpret our joint repeated presence as an invitation, it seemed amusing to Dan, though alarming to me. Not alarming because of its orientation, I hasten to add, but because it was a form of being *noticed*. The Invisible Other outside the door, whose imaginary presence I had to defeat, was briefly an actual Other, right there beside us, with an eyebrow pleasantly raised.

————

Dan had outgrown my self-frightened idea of "shame" and thought that shame itself—physical shame—was the shameful burden we bore, by choice. I began to understand that the therapy he offered his patients was the therapy not just of "acceptance" but of embracing one's own existence as a mammal with mammalian appendages, traduced by human anxieties. No shame in public bathrooms, no disgust to be found in shared urinals, no embarrassment in an embarrassing apparatus—a urinary aid called the Stadium Pal that he occasionally took on planes. Nothing human is alien to human beings, or ought to be. "Everybody is struggling with *something*" was his oft-repeated and undeniably true maxim, sometimes shortened to "Everybody's got something." Look around a subway car on a weekday morning, and there—apart from those obviously struggling with the crueler and more resistant mental disorders—invisible to our observing eye, was a man with a desperate fear of heights; a woman with chronic insomnia and another whose struggles with obsessive-compulsive disorder had been gratefully reduced to an intolerance for seeing a volume level on her iPhone at anything but an even number; a boy who lived in fear of choking; a ten-year-old girl sure she might be going blind; and a brilliant and accomplished professional with claustrophobia sufficient to leave him in daily terror of one day being forced inside an MRI machine.

It was Dan's task to show that we are part of a brotherhood and sisterhood of suffering, and that, even if this was a special by-product of living in a metropolitan, overstressed civilization—though there was no particular evidence to suggest that this was so, that New Yorkers were any more stressed out than those hunter-gatherers looking for the snake among the sticks—still, it includes millions. It was Dan's work to make one aware that, just as we are all in search of some kind of mastery in our hard-to-master lives, we are also all being pursued by one monster or another, with the fiendish, deeper defining truth that the monsters imitate the masters in their work. Our inner monsters construct those huge, Mordor-esque towers of anxiety in which we are imprisoned and which look so impressive that we easily mistake them for the more solidly constructed houses of accomplishment.

We can get out if we choose to. We can leave them if we want to. We built them in the first place.

———

THE IRONY OF riding my bike across the city to meet with Dan was evident to me, if not perhaps to him. Biking across town was, objectively, a far riskier thing to do than peeing in a public washroom. This was a case where the genuine difficulty was also, in plain fact, reasonably dangerous. The coping mechanism was likely to run me full tilt into an oncoming bus. It was a classic avoidance strategy—but one, ironically, of the Freudian kind, where avoiding the natural impulse creates the space for a civilized accomplishment. In this case, it was living more fully in the city I loved than I ever had before. I had sublimated my anxieties into a complementary activity, which didn't help cure them but did help to obscure them from my view for a while each day. Biking became my delight, my challenge, my exhilaration, my release, my relief. "Don't you feel young and free when you're biking?" Dan asked me innocently one day. It was true. I did feel young when doing it.

On one of those days, Dan suggested that we jump on our bikes and race down along the Hudson River to Hudson Yards, the new and much maligned hive of buildings that was part of the now dubious-seeming Bloomberg legacy to the city. Dan had started practicing there, but I had never been, partly on snobbish grounds, partly because it was a long way from home. But the bike ride there was exhilarating, as promised, down along by the aircraft carrier and the boats and the ever-beautiful river. Then, to my frightened disbelief whisking across the West Side Highway—yes, with the lights, but still—and on to the big complex of buildings.

We locked up our bikes—interesting that the metaphor of not being able to perform was derived from a practice in itself self-securing—and entered together. Up an escalator and into the main atrium. Wow! This place really was a mall, making the Time Warner Center look like a halfhearted, apologetic, don't-take-us-too-seriously attempt at one. Its four stories were filled with all the classic mall stores and dotted with adaptations and offshoots of more local New York ones, like Li-Lac Chocolate and William Greenberg Desserts.

Dan had a different revelation. "*Look* at this place!" he said, a kind of awe wreathing his words as he gazed up and around its many levels. "It's a kind of a paradise of washrooms. There's every kind of men's room you can practice in: big six and sixes, smaller three and threes. There's even on the third level, there's even a single unit with a single stall that you can actually lock, in case you have one of those days where you can't manage. You can find everything you need to practice in this one complex." So, we practiced, as variously as two men newly arrived in heaven, testing the harps.

————

HOW AM I DOING? The process, and the practice, continues. Mastery seems far off, still. I have surprised myself with capacity in places, like restaurants, long banished, and have disappointed myself—though not my therapist—with failures on the two airplane trips I've taken. On one I texted Dan, in the midst of a panic attack. "You may have some discomfort. But you're in no danger," he wrote back, laconically but empathetically. That distinction, between discomfort and danger, carried me over seven hours, and the eventual arrival at the London hotel.

I continue, twice a week, to bike to his place, then to bike to Hudson Yards to practice, and then, on a couple of memorable occasions, to bike all the way back home, seventy or so blocks— up the avenues, across the numbered streets, around buses and in front of trucks. Each ride, I am reminded of the irony, almost unbearable had it not been so delightful, that Dan had empowered me to do something that was in fact extremely dangerous while I was still struggling to do something that is not dangerous at all. Central Park West is full of memorials to fallen bicyclists, while the streets have no solemn statues to those who could not pee on planes. The release and loft of the accomplishment was enough to justify the risk. My groin was still enchained by its mysteries, but my feet were free to pedal all over town. It seemed a decent bargain to have made with the monster.

The Sixth Mystery
of Mastery

Catching the Bullet, or,
The Mystery of the Act Itself

S O WE HAVE NOW COUNTED UP MANY MYSTERIES of mastery: the mystery of intention and of judging intentions, the mystery of interiority, how we feel power and loss inside, the mystery of meaning and how we arrive at it, and even the mystery of prostheses and how we can be seduced, even misled, by them. But beyond all these is the simplest mystery of all, the easiest to execute, and the hardest to transcend, and that is the mystery of the act itself.

I watched my own son, at thirteen, become a petit maître, a small master, of card magic, one of the most fascinating things that you can possibly master. Eventually, Luke became skilled enough at card magic to find work over the summer as a personal assistant for David Blaine. He would come home with wonderful tales of Russian models and Indian fakirs and the intense consultations among professional magic advisors that precedes any stunt. It seemed that he was learning far more about life than he might in school.

At one point, Blaine had decided, for his next television spectacular, after doing his "sleepless" act, to do the "bullet catch." This is, as I've described, a famous old stunt in which, as the name suggests, a magician places a cup in his mouth and catches a bullet fired at him from across the stage. It had, I knew, been popular once on the vaudeville stage and just as dangerous as it sounds. At least six, perhaps as many as twelve, magicians had been killed onstage trying to perform the bullet catch, including William Robinson, aka the famous Chung Ling Soo, who died onstage when a blank became a real bullet. (Rumor had it that it was a deliberate act of revenge by Ching Ling Foo, an actual Chinese magician from whom Robinson had lifted the name and performance style. But this seems, perhaps unsurprisingly, untrue.)

Luke explained that Blaine was going to do the *real* bullet catch, not a gaffed version, of the kind that Penn & Teller accomplish onstage, with typical wit and irony, in which the spectator is led to believe that a real bullet is being fired and trapped while a blank is substituted. Alarmed, I asked him what the trick was to the bullet catch.

He paused. "Well, it's a small-caliber bullet, and a low-velocity rifle, and the cup is made of titanium and the shot is laser guided."

"So, there's no trick to the bullet catch?" I asked.

"Oh, yes, there's a trick to the bullet catch," he said instantly.

"What is it?" I asked.

"Dad, the trick to the bullet catch is catching the bullet," he replied.

I needed no more explanation. The trick to the bullet catch is *always* catching the bullet—trusting to your preparation and self-confident belief, your assistants and the bullet you chose. No matter how impeccably all of this may have been practiced and arranged, eventually the magician would have to turn toward the rifle with a cup lodged in his mouth and ask them to fire. The act of catching the bullet was a reflection of all those weeks—years, truly—of preparation, but, still, the bullet would have to be faced and caught, and this was not an act of derring-do or even of courage as we normally think of it. It was the instantaneous leap after a long sequence of planning. We have to pack our own parachutes with the silk that we have gathered and tested, probing it for each possible moth hole and tear . . . but then you have to jump out of the plane. The real work always comes down to a punctum, a small, distinct point, of choice and action. It may be overtly daring, or only implicitly so—no riskier, perhaps, than the lecturer's decision to speak without notes—but facing an audience, we are always catching the bullet.

This is the ultimate, or the final, truth of mastery. After all the preparation, all the work, all the double blinds and the doubling backs and the misdirections and the breaking down and building back up, we have to confront the thing itself, the fact of necessity, the leap of performance, the need to act.

No one who has ever done anything fails to see the point and the power of Luke's story. The trick to the bullet catch is catching the bullet. The mysterious hiss of atmospheric heat from the audience that greets the opening number of the musical show is the sound of the bullet escaping the barrel. Sooner or later, there is nothing between the performer and her performance. It doesn't matter if it's seen or not seen, big-time or small-time, fine or not. It has to happen. The space between thinking and happening is the biggest space of all.

Some have tried to make an entire worldview out of that metaphoric moment of the bullet catch, sufficient to live, or sometimes die, by. It's inherent in the theory of life that we call, crudely, "existentialism," meaning some synthesis—or, perhaps, some unduly forced reduction—of religious and metaphysical

European thinkers, from Kierkegaard to Heidegger and beyond to Jean-Paul Sartre and Camus. In an absurd universe, we have no choice but to take a leap toward faith and the irrational. It carries with it a rejection of the normal, the quotidian, the earthbound. Leap toward the Divine, we're told, or stay down here maundering with the rest of us.

The man who is perhaps first among my intellectual heroes, the French writer of the 1940s and '50s, Albert Camus, is sometimes taken to be a thinker of this kind, making this recommendation. His most forceful aphorism—"We must imagine Sisyphus happy!"—is read as a mordant gesture toward the impossibility of meaningful action. Sisyphus rolls the stone up the hill all day . . . it comes crashing down again just as it reaches the peak. What feels like effort is only futility, and we delude ourselves into the belief that it counts.

But for me, this has always been a misreading of Camus's point. We must imagine Sisyphus *happy*. Because while the only kind of action we can attempt may be illusory, a stone rolled up a hill only to roll down again, the happiness it gives us is not. Sisyphus is right to be happy with his work. It's what he's got. It's what *we* have. In a doomed, fatal, mortal world, we are all Sisyphus rolling stones, but we are also aware of the possibility of contentment as we do, not because the stone won't roll back (eventually, it will), but because when it does—and this is the secret, hopeful side to the curse that the gods gave Sisyphus—it doesn't actually crush us. It just gives us the work to do again.

Camus wrote once: "I don't know whether this world has a meaning that transcends it. But I know that I do not know that meaning and that it is impossible for me just now to know it. What can a meaning outside my condition mean to me? I can understand only in human terms. What I touch, what resists me—that is what I understand."

What I touch, what resists me. There are things that I can manage, and things I can't. But all of them are real. Camus's point is not that there is some hysterical leap to be made toward irrational faith, but that, in a universe where meaning is something we make up, not something we're given, we're right to turn to the material, the tangible, exactly, to the real.

For the simple magicians' phrase "the real work" carries within it a quiet pun. On the one hand it references authenticity, authority, accomplishment. But it can take place only within an orbit of actual things and practices. One of the reasons that we are so moved by the virtuosity of fingers and feet, by magic and music-making, even more than we are by the intensity of minds, by philosophy or even literature, is that they remind us of the irreducible element of sheer physicality in their construction. They're not just real, they're work. They are as fragile as our bones are. Mastery is emphatically not "transcendent," not something that one can glimpse in an epiphany or see in a vision.

Even spiritual mastery, as the Zen writers tell us, begins with chopping wood and drawing water. Mastery demands hard, solid things that have to be prepared, parachutes that have to be packed, acts that have to be enacted. We stare down the barrel of the rifle that our sterling (*we hope?*) assistant has packed with the right (*we believe . . .*) small-caliber bullet while feeling the solid and unbreakable (*we're confident!*) cup between our teeth and face the world. The trick to the bullet catch is catching the bullet. The bad news is that there's no escaping the necessity. The good news is that the bullet can be caught.

The Real Work,
in Progress

Boxing and Dancing

None of our hearts are pure, we always have mixed
    motives,
Are self-deceivers, but the worst of all
Deceits is to murmur 'Lord, I am not worthy'
And, lying easy, turn your face to the wall.
But may I cure that habit, look up and outwards
And may my feet follow my wider glance
First no doubt to stumble, then to walk with the others
And in the end—with time and luck—to dance

                —Louis MacNiece, *Autumn Journal*

J OEY CONTRADA, MY BOXING TEACHER, HAS THE
most extraordinary face I've ever seen. His wide-open eyes,
crowning his narrow, high-cheekboned features, seem permanently caught in a state of startled disbelief. At first, I thought
this might be startled disbelief at the sight of a boxing student
as awkward as I am. But I came to realize that it was an almost
fixed reaction, a sense of wonder and slight awe at existence itself.
He has the same look on his face when he batters an opponent
into submission on the many YouTube videos he stars in, and the

same look when he instructs nine-year-old girls in the act of what we dumb Westerners call kickboxing. He is, according to one law of accomplishment, a teacher amazed by his students.

A Muay Thai fighter, he has been, as he modestly insists, merely an amateur champion, a junior welterweight star of a popular New York promotion called "Friday Night Fights." Not the most impressive-sounding title, perhaps, but, just as the unknown chess players at the French café who played inside the Turk represented a huge class of strong players, there is more than enough Muay Thai mastery among the Manhattan millions to make their champ a *champ*. Watching him on YouTube amazed me. For my part, I had, after years of dutiful New York rituals of weightlifting, been urged to meet with him. "You'd like boxing," a friend had said, measuring not my natural affinity for quick-twitch slugging, but a hard core of competitiveness that might drive me forward.

I did find it appealing, instantly, partly out of family nostalgia, partly out of literary association, and partly out of some still unsublimated, unworthy curiosity about what it might be like actually to be able to slug somebody and watch them fall down. The family nostalgia was rooted in memories of my grandfather, and even of my father. My grandfather loved boxing. It was his one sport, his favorite sport, his only sport. A small man, like everyone in my family, he had an impressive barrel chest and biceps so swelling that he could actually make them dance, shimmying them up and down as though bouncing to an exotic beat, for the (actually quite frightened) amusement of his eight grandchildren.

When I was a child, he had instructed me regularly in the history of fighting, both the microhistory of his own, and the macrohistory of his period. When he arrived in "this country" in the

1920s, already mature at the age of twelve, he brought with him the schoolyard fighting styles of the Old Country. "You'd take off your belt and swing it at the other fella," he explained. His first day at an American school, in Philadelphia, the other kids said, "You can't do that here! You can't fight with a belt buckle! Get your fists up!" He was both bemused by the nicety in what was, after all, a primitive dust-up, and ready to learn the new cultural lesson. So, he put his fists up and fought.

In the macrohistory, it was Benny Leonard, the great Jewish lightweight of the teens and '20s, who was first among his heroes. He spoke of him often: his jab, his intelligence, his canny craft. "I watched him, how he never got touched . . . backed off and then came forward." (I was never clear if he had seen Leonard fight, which seemed a bit improbable, given the realities of a working-class existence on the Philadelphia docks—selling fish, not moving cargo—or merely thought that he had seen him from hearing about him so often, a synesthetic transfer from knowledge to images that, as in music, is psychologically easy.)

We are now the masters of much of the past, at least much more than our grandfathers, to a degree that we enjoy the whole of it on YouTube . . . and while we do enjoy it, we hardly yet have registered it adequately as a truth of our lives. It's all there! And there, at the touch of a tab, he was: Benny Leonard, fighting in the 1920s. Watching him, I nearly burst out in grateful laughter. His body was not my grandfather's solid wrestler's body, made of schmalz and gristle—no, it was *my* body. Or a variant of it. There he was, a little Jewish guy with sharp features and a receding hairline and scraggly legs and a sunken chest and barely visible biceps. His were, I realized, the days before body building and weight training, before grilled-protein diets and carb-loading, much less steroids and performance-enhancing pills and creams. Benny Leonard's was a body you would see now in the locker room of a New York gym, worn by an eagle eyed and cynical accountant, by a lawyer. He was not a Jewish athlete in the idealized manner of Philip Roth's virtuous life-guard in *Nemesis*, admirably muscled and impressive. No, this guy, the greatest Jewish fighter, belonged to a time even before that, to the generation of Roth's father, not his brothers. His nameless opponents were no buffer, and so the fights looked exactly as if you had taken two little hungry guys out of the old William Morris Agency and told them to strip down to their boxers and start slugging each other. (Which, I suspect, they would happily have done.)

But even I could sense, through the old jerky, black-and-white action, the speed and thrift with which he pursued his opponent, hands darting, arms pressed out. Above all, there was his obvi-ous skill in retreat: balding head snapping out of harm's way, long skinny legs—well, not dancing, exactly, as with the great Black boxers, but retreating, even if the movement was less syncopated shuffling than rapid backpedaling.

Speed! But Jewish speed, as I couldn't help but think of it, the speed of self-preservation extended out over the millennia. Leonard's scurrying wasn't evasive speed but escape speed: get outta there, fast. I had some of the doubtless dubious affection for the idea of a Jewish boxer that others might have for Jew-ish gangsters—dubious because there is no particular virtue in being good at violent things, even if it seems to go against type.

By far the best account of Benny Leonard, both of his mys-tique and of his fighting style, I discovered, is by Budd Schul-berg in one of his collections of boxing pieces. Schulberg, to my mind, may be the most underrated of all American authors, the author of the best firsthand account of F. Scott Fitzgerald, in his novel *The Disenchanted*, and the inventor of a permanent American kind, Sammy Glick, in *What Makes Sammy Run?* Curiously, his reputation has descended to a more blue-collar, artisanal role, known now only for things like the screenplay of *On the Waterfront*. Glamour attaches to writers haphazardly; some craftsmen get elevated to become cult heroes, like the noir writer David Goodis, and some real writers descend to be treated as blue-collar literary lounge magicians, hardworking and helpful but not really ready for the big rooms. Schulberg, in any case, writes about the fundamentally *verbal* nature of Leonard's supremacy, bantering with his Italian and Irish opponents.

Leonard would taunt: "'You got my hands down, what do you wanna bet you can't hit me? Come on, if you think you've got me hurt, why don't you fight? You look awful slow to me, Richie, looks like you're getting tired . . .'" As Schulberg decides, "That round had been more of a debate than a boxing match, with Benny winning the verbal battle and Richie swinging wildly and futilely as he tried to chop Benny down." There was something irresistible about the existence of a great fighter who tried to argue his opponents out of their trunks and onto the canvas. The boxing bug that had infected my grandfather had even infected his infinitely more literary and intellectual son, my father, who became the first university graduate in his family, at Penn (in the days before attending an "Ivy" was as big a deal as it has since become; it was the good local Philadelphia school) and went on to spend his life teaching Richardson and Fielding and Molière. But when the 1976 Olympics came to Montreal, he got tickets for all the boxing matches, and we saw Sugar Ray Leonard defeat a young Cuban boxer with a TKO to grab the gold medal. But, rewatching the fight on the internet I also noted, as Howard Cosell had at the time, announcing the match, how beautifully Sugar Ray danced, circled, to his left to cut down the angles, as purposeful as he was graceful—a Black Benny, his odd namesake, in every way.

———

So Saturday after Saturday I took the subway out to a little gym in Queens—Hines Combat, beautifully found just half a block east and below the elevated tracks of the F trains, one of the last old-fashioned elevateds in the city. It gave the place a certain Ben Shahn grace. Inside there was a flurry of flying fists and high-kicking nine-year-old girls.

Joey put me to work at once, shortly after the kids' class ended, teaching me my fighting stance, one leg back, the other forward. And then a pattern of punches: two left jabs, turned inward, fists made properly, with the thumb curled over the knuckles, then the right cross, made by shifting weight onto the right leg, and turning the right foot almost vertical to assure the shift.

Then, as in subsequent weeks, he put me to work shadowboxing in front of the mirror. Two left jabs, then a right cross, over and over and over. Two left jabs, then a right cross—"Jab! Jab! Now cross." Simple as it seemed it was, as much as Jacob's tilts in time, subject to immense refinement, many necessary adjustments, shadings of intention and meaning. The jab had to be thrown, not merely extended; it needed to twist as it "landed," for maximum effect; the cross, far from being a mere extension of the upper body, had to begin—had to!—in the right leg, the fighter's whole focus on turning the foot straight up and outward to be sure that the punch was rising from the hip and lower body, turning as in a comic-book blow—POW!—not merely being weakly pushed forward from the shoulder. Just as important, the cross had to be "hidden" behind the jab so that it came as a sneaky surprise right after the jab had been blocked by the opponent: bad news caught; worse news delivered.

Most important of all, the hands had to spring back instantly to guard the head, the punch scarcely thrown before the need to protect against the return blow. The constant frightened cycle had to be imprinted on your body—throw and guard, throw and guard. The propelling emotion was not aggression but its opposite: a watchful and wary defensive awareness.

Joey stopped as I caught my breath—despite cycling, post-Dan, ten miles a day in Central Park, no breathless is as breathless as ten minutes of high-spirited shadowboxing—and discussed with me the various ways in which the hands can be used to encase the head: the classic manner in which they make a visible block, and the radical Cus D'Amato manner, passed on to Floyd Patterson and eventually Mike Tyson, where the hands are planted at the side of the head and the fighter pulls back from the approaching blows to the nose—which seemed unpromising for someone like me who was frightened even of a phantom punch from a nonexistent opponent. (I was to learn that to reduce the D'Amato system to the hands and head was like reducing Shakespeare's "system" to having ten syllables in each line, or the Bill Walsh West Coast offense to "short passes," but that came later.)

Joey continued pressing the simple act of left jab, right cross, and then, a week or two later, added to the sequence a short left hook and then two uppercuts, left and right. A sequence that I had watched repeated many times in the boxing ring was not an improvisation, or even a ritualized probing. It was a plan. More than a plan, it was a scheme—a series of tricks, just like a shuffle in Erdnase. *Watch my left, now watch it again, it's annoying, ha! While you were misdirected there, I sneak the right cross in behind it.*

And then, when you go to dodge that, why, the left hook emerges to bash you sideways!

The beauty of the sequence, of course—with which in my imagination I was felling my overconfident, bemuscled, loutish Bluto-esque opponent—could not entirely conceal the truth that, so well-rehearsed, it would have been as transparent to my opponent as Steve Forte insists Erdnase's stock shuffle was to the other card players in the smoking car. He could see it coming. *Boy*, he could see it coming! I pointed this out, jocularly, to Joey, but he took the point very seriously.

"Yeah. He can see it coming. But we're trying to get him into a state of reflex and reaction rather than thinking. So, he just puts up his defenses and moves instinctively. That's our opportunity. We're trying to have you thinking just one split second ahead of his reflexes. That's where the mind's advantage is in fighting. We want you not thinking, just reacting. But we want his reacting to be reacting to your thinking." It was a complex formula of blows thrown, thoughts meditated upon, and then reactions, punches threaded like charms on a chain of meta-concerns. Once again, something as simple seeming as a series of punches was a complicated, inward-turning Möbius strip encompassing your intention, another mind's guess at your intention, your getting sufficiently ahead of the other mind so as to frustrate the guess, and the other mind's not being quick enough to get ahead of your getting ahead, with the punch landing only at the end of all of that. I had learned, on the stages of musical theatre and cabaret, that excellence among performers didn't rely on their being "in tune" with the audience but rather always a minute, sometimes only a moment, ahead of them, offering a series of small explosions of surprise. (Vulgar performers make the surprises obvious; dull ones never surprise at all.) In the ring, you had to be one thought ahead of the man who was trying to hit you, even when the ring existed only in your head and Joey's gesture.

Over time, I got to know Joey a bit. Behind his astonished stare, he turned out to be one of those wonderfully self-educated men who had risen upward and outward from a blue-collar Italian Irish background in Boston, having found as his guidebook, as so many have, Joseph Campbell's *Hero with a Thousand Faces*. The ideas there stirred and motivated him: above all the notion that the hardest way was the best way, and that "the cave you fear to enter holds the treasure you seek." He worked as a DJ in New York and then stumbled into a Muay Thai gym in lower Manhattan. Electrified, as so many young fighters have been before by the mental discipline of martial arts, the heroic sublimation of violence into systematic self-denial, the achievement of character by controlling your own capacity for taking pain and inflicting punishment, he began to train. "Finally, my teacher told me I was ready for a fight. I was terrified! I mean, terrified. And then when I stepped into the ring . . . I wasn't afraid. I said, Is this okay, that I'm not afraid? He said it was."

Muay Thai fighting is what Americans call, sloppily, kickboxing, the form of native Thai "martial arts" that involves several striking surfaces, many more than in Western boxing: elbows, knees, the sides of the foot, as much as if not more than fists. It makes for spectacular YouTube footage at its peak, when one right spinning kick meets one vulnerable jaw, though in extended sequence it can be surprisingly dull, as the two fighters collapse together in one corner of the ring, pummeling with elbows and short squallish kicks, tenderizing each other's flesh. In Joey's teaching, he focused increasingly on throwing punches, on the boxing side, partly because that's what his students were interested in and partly because the truth, as he confided in me, is that throwing punches is a more effective way of inflicting a concussion on someone else than kicking is.

There is within that reality one of the effective constraints of physicality to consider. In truth, human beings are better with their hands and arms than we are with our feet. Our evolutionary specialty was not walking but throwing. We're good at it in ways that none of the other nearly bipedal creatures are. This is one more of the physical constraints that can cut both ways: we have throwing sports, including the throwing sport of boxing . . . and yet the world's most popular sport is soccer, exactly because it evens out our skills, using the thing we're less naturally good at, and compels us to learn a set of skills that are antithetical, or at least at right angles, to our physiology. You get good at bending balls and making passes and *are* good at throwing fastballs. (You can get better at that, too, but the activity is uniquely human.)

Spear throwing and punching seem, at least, to have evolved together. It's not an accident that we talk of "throwing a punch." And while one should touch all evolutionary speculation with a ten-foot spear, or fend it off with a long left jab, it does seem that human physiognomy, particularly of the testosterone-fueled kind, is peculiarly well designed for throwing punches—though whether this would be for the ends of sexual selection, displayed, so to speak, in a human "lek," or mating ritual, or for actual hierarchy climbing, punching your way to the top of the tribe, is hard to know. Once spears and swords are on the scene, as they have been for a very long time, in evolutionary measure, throwing punches necessarily takes a secondary, recreational, symbolic role. Boxing is, and always has been it seems, a spectacle first, a form of assault only in the absence of a weapon. (The natural human thing to do is swing a belt buckle.)

After six weeks or so with Joey, I went back to watch Benny

Leonard. My slightly sharpened understanding—still almost unimaginably far from mastery—showed me how skilled he really was, once one truly saw past the surprising soft surface of his body and the unapologetic ordinariness of his physique. He used his jab as a weapon, darting it out and turning it perfectly, and used it, too, as a defensive object holding off an opponent, even at times, sneakily wrapping it around the trusting Irishman or Italian, seeming to whisper in his ear, only to land a few sharp right undefended (and indefensible) hooks. His left jab was a thing of beauty: a dagger of assault; a shield; a sneak attack. And he moved sideways so well, slipping and making the turn! He was a hero to me, as he had been to prior Gopnik men.

The tale of ethnic-ordeal-by-athletic-contest is so deeply implanted in the American imagination that it is nearly irresistible. DiMaggio showed all those Italian-haters that Italians weren't all gangsters and fruit-stall vendors (but did many people really think they were?) and Benny Leonard that Jews weren't cowards. (But who exactly thought *that*?) The literally millions of Italians and Jews and Irish who, in the nature of things, have to get along and did, on the streets of eastern cities, with ethnic friction usually not raised beyond the range of a chafing tease, hardly seems in need of this auto-da-fé. But we want it anyway, presumably working backward: having the ethnic athletic hero alone isn't enough unless it gets attached to some larger social act of vengeance. The real American weakness is not for ethnic hatred but for larger points. Just watching one guy hit another skillfully is hardly enough. Schulberg reports "You killed our Christ!" was the accusation that Leonard heard throughout his youth. That he could knock down Catholic boys was hardly proof that we hadn't, but it at least suggested that there was more to the subject than might appear.

"Respect," the primitive form of inter-ethnic honor, is not an entirely dismissible emotion. We really *do* want respect. Ritualized conflict is one way to earn it.

———

I DISCOVERED IN MYSELF a deep affection for the art of fist-fighting, entirely abstract and independent of any actual experience of throwing a fist in a fight. A print addict since I was four, by now words have insidiously repopulated my ganglions and synapses, and so the experience of the words has replaced, not merely supplemented, experience. Everything passes through language. Which is to say: I loved the literature of boxing almost more than I loved boxing. Reading about fights ancient and modern, from Pierce Egan through the sainted Joe Liebling to lesser artists, I recognized a uniquely appealing literary subject. Direct combat between two minimally protected opponents, without support of armor, and not mimic combat either as in tennis or, God help us, golf. Even nine-year-olds boxing showed the same currents of crisis, the same shaped combat, that makes the encounters of Achilles and Hector in the *Iliad* still hyper-gripping to read about.

We are told, by writers more ingenuous than me, and certainly all much better punchers, that it is the isolation and self-dependence of the writer that leads him—and latterly, her—so often to the ring. We make our destinies alone, facing the page, as the boxer makes his, facing the opponents. We engage in an existential act, facing our fears, pummeling our nightmares, catching the bullet. But surely the writing life in most respects the opposite of the fighter's and what draws us is the more frequent magnetic power of the opposite pole. To actually act out, to make a mental preparation into a single strong physical gesture, to throw a punch—to catch the bullet by actually catching one, or as near to it as one could hope to experience, a blow to the head being as hard a bullet as one would want—has the appeal of the one thing writers never have, and that is decisive experience.

A writer's experience of writing is deliberative. No matter how much we may try to find a stunt that will make it flow—automatic writing, or midnight inspiration—finally the element of deliberation will always return and triumph. We make drafts. We take time. We choose words. We chew pencils. If boxers actually fought the way that writers write, they would be stopping in the middle of every round to rethrow the same punch in six nearly but not quite identical ways, then turn to their spouse, seated at ringside, to ask if that seemed like a better version, what do you think? It's better, right? No, hold on, I have still another to share, watch *this* . . . Condemned to a life of deliberated action, authors dream of direct and decisive experience, and then, having immersed themselves in someone else's direct experience, pretend that they have had that too.

Why did I want to box? In another way, the literary connection was in itself an encouragement toward an inquiry into what I suppose I have to call masculinity. There was within me a certain amount of unassimilated anger, and so, however hoary it may seem now, a certain curiosity about courage. The old Hemingway and Mailer obsessions with asserting masculinity—a theatrical gesture with the older writer, an existential one with the younger—was not entirely dismissible, any more than the question of ethnic honor had been in the past. It was not entirely without presence in my heart.

I had written often about Hemingway, admiringly, and had actually met Mailer once over dinner, where, me still a youngster, we had been seated together. Excited at the idea, I was sure

I would encounter the subtle, serious novelist who lived beneath the cheap, talk-show pugilist and Elaine's existentialist—a role, I was sure, cannily deployed to keep the book advances fluffed up, with the constant feuds and scandals that seemed, to my doubtless too monotonous and monogamous generation, embarrassing.

Not a bit of it. He played the Mailer part. "Have you been following my feud with the feminists?" was, truly, the first thing he said, and then: "You know what I call them? Wo-wos. Because they've taken the 'man' out of woman." It was if one sat down with Elmer Fudd in a duplex on Central Park West, expecting at last to meet the real man behind the hat and rifle, and heard him talk all night about how pwetty soon, he would get that cwazy wabbit. Celebrity is indeed a mask that eats into the face, as John Updike, a wiser writer, once remarked. But then Updike was a golfer.

And the literary life imagined as a boxing arena has a nearly Dante-like cost: you get punch-drunk young. Neither Mailer nor Hemingway had written anything really first-rate and characteristic after fifty; seeing writing as a series of bouts turns it into a series of competitive bouts and one thing that happens in competitive bouts is that you get drained. Writers who lasted treated writing less like fighting and more like farming, a fallow season followed by a replanting and then another harvest. Though both had late successes it was only with what I think of as replica books, *The Old Man and the Sea* and *The Executioner's Song*, worthy efforts that impressed reviewers, as reviewers are always impressed, with an unexpected minimalism after the garrulous past, but which but weren't close to the core of their real, expansive talents.

It is curious to think that modern American literature begins in effect with two fables of tough-seeming Jews who aren't what they seem: with Hemingway in *The Sun Also Rises*—in a way whose awfulness has only become apparent in our time—that the pitiful Robert Cohn, based on the writer Harold Loeb, despite having been a boxing champion at Princeton, was unworthy of the lady Brett. Cohn's pretensions to manliness, by way of having been a boxer, albeit the Ivy League kind, are empty Jewish affectations, compared to the true aficon of the narrator and his non-Jewish buddies.

Fitzgerald, meanwhile, turned the obviously Jewish tough boy, intimate (or is it errand boy?) of Arnold Rothstein, Jimmy Gatz, into the fake WASP Gatsby. Gatsby's Jewishness is much argued over, though it makes sense of Tom Buchannan's announced allegiance to extreme right-wing racial systems—the intention, the subcurrent throughout, is that part of the panic Gatsby creates in Buchanan's mind is that he *might* be Jewish. ("We don't know anything about him," Tom says.) The transformations, the threat of the Jews is always not that they can't be assimilated but that they *can*—that they will pass, they will be sneaky enough to get by when "our" guard is down, and pass as fighters, pass as millionaires, pass as lovers of our Daisys, pass as writers. Antisemitism has at its heart the constant threat of Jewish assimilation into some other form—into heroism, or American athleticism, or French patriotism, or into "whiteness." The Jew is not only, in antisemitic imagination, an obstinate partisan of his own kind, like Shylock, but also the eternal shapeshifter who can never be trusted. Fitzgerald, to his credit, gives his creation a romantic grandeur at the end, but, as perhaps generations of readers have missed, the reluctance with which he confesses this admiration—the truth that his admiration has to be confessed, not boasted of—is in part a function of how much ethnic-racial dissembling has to precede it. You shouldn't like Gatz/Gatsby, he's part of Wolfsheim's mob, but you do. He might even pass as a boxer in the ring.

———

BOXING, IT TURNED OUT, at least my kind of boxing, shadowboxing in front of a gym mirror in Queens and then pummeling the pads that Joey held up for me, shouting out the order of blows like a square-dance caller—"Double jab!" "Cross!" "Double jab, cross, hook, right uppercut!"—was far removed from even the most minimal encounter with courage, other than that necessary to ride the subway in the pandemic era. The entire enterprise was geared to an imaginary opponent who would never arrive—not unless I suddenly needed a payday and there suddenly appeared to contest the prize a string of pint-size, over-sixty lightweight Muay Thai fighters. Short of that, the other fighter at whom the whole enterprise was directed would never arrive at all.

Showing courage was less important to boxing than inventing fear—investing the nonexistent opponent against whom one is shadowboxing with sufficient smarts and violence to keep one's hands springing back to the sides of your head. "He'll get me if I don't watch out!" was more important in Joey's learning system than "Take that, you cur!" All systems of accomplishment are in one sense defensive systems—it was exactly Arturo's noodle that one had to be in order to box. Not following a path forward but turning your head defensively was at the heart of both systems.

Over time, new things were added to the scheme Joey taught me, but the underlying motif of short, repeated actions was unchanging. Joey introduced me to the work of Alexis Arguello, the great and tragic Nicaraguan fighter, who in the 1970s and early '80s fought and won championships in three weight classes. He was Joey's hero—he kept a picture of him near his bed—and, studying Arguello's fights on YouTube as well, I soon saw why. He was a master, a perfect "technical" fighter, the sweet science crystallized. Arguello was famous for the piston-like precision of his punching, but I recognized, through Joey, that Arguello's gift was actually for *not* punching—for *withdrawing* his hands, getting back into perfect defensive posture almost the moment he had thrown a punch, which left him safe to throw another. The seemingly passive act was the accomplished act—the self-discipline to focus on not throwing, to leap your right hand back by the side of your head the microsecond after you had thrown it out. It is the equivalent of the comping of a great musician. Half the joy of hearing a pianist like Bill Evans or a guitarist like Jim Hall is to hear them *not* playing at their best. There is so much mastery in their hands and minds that when they are not playing at their best they are playing even better. The abbreviated, encoded version of the chords they clock is as thrilling as the virtuoso solos. The power is all in reserve. Arguello was like that.

Tragic, I should add, because after his fighting days were done he leapt into Nicaraguan politics, became disillusioned with the Sandinistas, and then committed suicide. And also because his most famous loss came in a fight with Aaron Pryor, in which Pryor's trainer famously called out, between rounds, to "give me that other bottle, the one I mixed." Pryor, trailing on points, suddenly came back out to win the fight. (Joey and I, between "rounds," love to debate what was in the bottle.)

I learned to move sideways, hopping off to one side in order to cut down the angle and arrive, almost magically, given the galumphing way in which I did it, focused on the weak, undefended side of the imaginary opponent's head. Then the short hook would do him in. To the underlying grammar of *jab, jab, cross, hook*, Joey added *jab, jab, cross, hook . . . hop!* Then, again:

jab, cross, hook! The abrupt, telegraphic moves became, over time, a code imprinted on the mind. Rather like the Hare Krishna prayer, though with a different goal, not worldly transcendence in the arms of a Hindu god but landing a blow on another guy's nose, the words were repeated so often that they almost lost their familiar meaning, and became a hum, a set of seamless sounds sung to the Spirit of Boxing—in this case, intended to induce a concussion in a phantom. Over and over the same four-beat burst, like old-fashioned telegraphy, urgent as a shipboard SOS: *jab, jab, cross, hook! Jab, jab, cross, hook! Jab, jab, cross, hook . . .* step!—*jab, jab, cross, hook.* I loved being in that gym.

———

AS I LEARNED to box on Saturdays in Queens, my daughter, Olivia, and I were learning to dance on weekdays in Manhattan. Olivia had been the light of my eyes and romance of my existence since her birth in Paris twenty years before. Where her brother, Luke, had inherited his mother's graceful entries into the world and her contemplative nature—he was getting his PhD in philosophy in Austin, making ruminative notes on Longhorn games and Texas manners and on Derek Parfit's normative theories— she had taken on my horizontal, short-breathed mind, was splendid at scholarship, quick at conversation, good at any specific subject or practice she put her mind to. Having already scooted up a ladder of achievement, she was still searching, I thought, in a way I understood too well, for the one true accomplishment.

Amid her movement from achievement to achievement, Olivia had declared herself a lesbian—though "declare" or "announce" is the wrong verb there. The simple, settled verb sequence of "said that she was" captures it better. *She said that she was queer.* It was an undramatic event, more reassuring to her mother and to me than startling. Reassuring because so much of her life in high school had been spent, in the brutal way of our time, in trying to get into college, cracking the code of admissions offices: this item on your CV but not that one; bringing about peace in the Middle East by speaking fluent medieval Arabic to both sides while playing saxophone in a suitably diverse bisexual band while maintaining an A average and still doing stand-up on Saturday nights in Brooklyn.

I had tried to insist, coming from an academic family as I did, on the perpetual truth of the Turk: that the player inside might be unknown to you and still be magnificent, meaning, in this case, that there were so many first-rate humanities PhDs emerging jobless from even the best universities—her brother well aware of this fact—that you were as likely to find that one great mentor in some obscure or "secondary" university as in the big-name ones. It was maybe *more* likely, since the big-name ones had grabbed the big names right after they had done something great that they would not do again. (Kurt Gödel, the greatest of all logicians, thought, logically, that the Institute of Advanced Study in Princeton was sure to fire him after hiring him in the 1940s, since they could see that he had done his best work in his twenties and nothing he did now was nearly as important. This was completely logical and, in its way, absolutely true, though of course it mistook the purpose of his being hired, which was to be a sign in the shop window luring in other scholars and students: he was there to serve the institute, not to do advanced study.)

Nothing doing. There was no convincing her not to try. And so, having submitted to the self-annihilating system, she emerged from it with the gold ring but without having had much of the kind of social activity that normal kids have in a normal high school. (Her mother, a maiden of Icelandic manners, had been happily involved with a boy at the age of fifteen.) So her discovering herself within the world of intimate relations was wonderful, and her girlfriend was a wonderful girl, smart and dear and touchingly attentive to Olivia's parents. All of it good, nothing but a plus.

And yet the question of achievement versus accomplishment hovered. The joy I had found in boxing—not in mastery of boxing, of course, but in the building up, bit by bit—was something I wanted to now share with her. (Though it was Olivia, it suddenly occurs to me who, before she went away to college, had actually been the first in our family to take up boxing, occasionally going downtown with a friend for determined lessons in determination.) One day I said to her, simply, "Olivia! Why don't we learn to dance together?" It seemed a way of untangling that complicated knot of "issues" that we shared. Somewhat to my surprise—she's a busy woman—she said yes, emphatically and instantly. "I'd love to do that, Dad! Let's do it, whenever we can!" I recognized in the alacrity of her acceptance, along with a touching generosity, some similar emotion to my own, a desire to lean into each other a little bit more and bounce off each other a little bit less. We never argued, but our exchanges tended to be on the cerebral edge, critic father to smart daughter. (One of her professors, in her first year in college, had written to her to warn her that they were reading a piece of mine in class and to ask if she was indeed a relation, given that they might well be critical of it. "Adam is my father," she had written back, "and I am often critical of him.")

Then, in her first published piece in the college newspaper, she had written, touchingly, of the difficulties she felt in experiencing, for the first time, things not shared with her mother, "The person in the world I'm closest to." I made a B-plot appearance with the line "the familiar sound of sports radio in the kitchen where my father cooked." "You threw me under the bus, baby!" I joked. "I'm just the hash-slinger in the kitchen making eggs and listening to *Mike and the Mad Dog*." Not an entirely false description, her immediately subsequent expression said, nor an entirely insulting one, since her favorite of my "bits" had always been that of the sports pair, saturnine, misanthropic Mike—"Well, that was the most asinine phone call we have had in months"—and hysterical Chris Russo—"Mike! I can't believe that caller!" And then there was the complexity that her mother, whom she loved, was a wonderful dancer, naturally graceful and lithe in movement, who had once thought of becoming a professional.

I went out to find a dance instructor and did. His name was Steve Dane, though I transposed it on my contacts to "Steve Dance." Though Olivia and I didn't know it then, we were blessed with an exceptional teacher. Steve Dane was actually, the glory of his near-miss name aside, the founder of the Manhattan Ballroom Society, and came from a long line of dancers: his grandmother taught dancing for more than half a century, and it was in Yonkers, at her studio, that Steve had begun to master dance. These days, he explained, much of his work was with couples about to get married, but his preservationist's passion for the beautiful old forms of dancing, waltzes and fox-trots, was evident even under his carefully controlled half smile. He was, physically, very nearly the opposite of Joey Contrada. Small and upright, where the boxer was gangly and long-limbed, he had a face that betrayed not astonishment but only a mild sardonic watchfulness, as though both restraining his love of dancing and disclosing a certain ironic recognition that teaching ballroom dancing was, really, too specialized a thing to have made into a life's work. His job mostly involved teaching those soon-to-be-married couples how to dance at their wedding—one of the few remaining moments when normal people are expected to engage in actual, formal dancing, rather than the kind of sluggish thrumming in space that passes for dancing in most of our social occasions now.

It was still the depths of the pandemic and so, feeling unsafe in any plan to meet indoors, he suggested meeting outside, on the long esplanade in Central Park that stands above the Wollman Rink, a place that, as it happened, Olivia and I had often shared in her childhood, when she took ice-skating lessons, not terribly successfully, but with maximum intensity. Many sites of her childhood were nearby, flooding me with emotion. There was the carousel where we had gone often in the hard months after 9/11, trying to replicate on its speedy revolving side the gentler experience her brother had had in the Luxembourg Gardens growing up. I kept a photograph of her on it on my desk.

Steve came, in shirt and tie, hyper-formal, as small, elegant men tend to be, and as befitted someone who was teaching dance. He brought a boombox with him of a kind I hadn't seen in the park since the '80s passed and the era of the kids arriving with boomboxes balanced on their shoulders, marking a form of loud aural possession of a patch of the park, had ended. They seem to have been swept away by the epoch of the earbuds. Steve put his boombox down, fiddled with the controls, and began to play . . . foxtrot music.

To my bliss, it was an old favorite: Sinatra singing "Fly Me to the Moon," with the Basie Orchestra, decorated with period jazz flute played by Frank Wess, the underknown reed player who more or less invented the sound of the jazz flute, a thing I had learned from the years when I edited Whitney Balliett's great jazz writing. (Trained as a flautist in a conservatory, Wess had made the jazz leap to tenor sax, only to keep the flute in his back pocket, so to speak, until, in the '60s, when Basie encouraged him to solo with it in place of his tenor. A '60s sound was born, of a mix of old practice, new opportunity, and surprising combination—one that by now I could recognize as almost a formula, the one true equation, of mastery itself.)

So, there was Sinatra, and the thump of the Basie band, and Frank Wess's long-delayed emancipation of his flute, and my baby daughter, all on the esplanade above the skating rink. As with every place in New York during the pandemic, a wary, jumpy peace reigned overall. Rats, who had been overwhelming the park since the pandemic began, could be sensed worryingly rustling and racing in the low bushes at the edge of the esplanade. People came and went in couples, almost all masked. We three people dancing to Sinatra at the end of the esplanade got basically no attention. Dan Rocker's hard-to-learn lesson—that no one really notices even eccentric behavior, that you can mostly follow your star, or your zipper, without raising the eyebrows or attention of the Others, who are following their own—was true here, as it is everywhere.

I did not know what the foxtrot was or even might be, aside from its generic use to mean "formal dancing" and its naughty double-entendre appearance in Sondheim's "Can That Boy Foxtrot." The real foxtrot, it turns out, is a dance as neatly ordered as, and with an odd resemblance to, the sequence of jabs and crosses and hops in the basic recipe of boxing. In the foxtrot, you hold your partner at arm's length—and suddenly the old term had new meaning! Arm's length not meaning at a disdainful distance, but at a respectful attention, one hand on her arm, the other around her back. Then, the man leading, you take a firm step forward with your left foot—like leading with the left jab, the weaker side doing the stronger work—and then with the right, the woman retreating by mimicking the same steps, and then brush the left foot sideways, stepping to the left and meeting your partner's eyes, once more in place.

It is a sequence, *exactly*, in simplicity and left-right patterning, in shifting weight and quick-following feet, like the jab-jab-cross system of boxing. Then, just as in the simplest fighting pattern you insert the sideways hop to the vulnerable side, in the foxtrot you stop and slide over—"slide" being the operative word, the necessary action, just as Arturo taught me about driving on the highway, a slide, slightly slurred, always being better than a leap or abruptness—and then gather in your partner. *Left, right, slide, left, right, slide.* Arm around your partner . . . Fly me to the moon! Let me swing among the stars!

"It is the *most* completely gendered activity in the world," Olivia said one night over dinner, when her mother pressed about our dance lessons. She was right, of course. The man leads, the woman follows. You step forward with your left foot; she retreats with her right. As you advance into the "promenade," she spins, and you step quick to catch her. Steve would often join us in these moments, making the twosome into a threesome—pressing on my back, encouraging me to lead, to be decisive in stepping forward and sideways with my partner.

The irony was that in boxing action was essentially defensive—you were always retreating from the enemy who does not exist or exists only in your mind—while it was in dancing that you had to assert yourself, step forward, lead. The combat sport was most wisely pursued from something close to a state of defensive paranoia; the social grace was best pursued as a series of aggressive actions.

"Of course, we could spin it around; you lead, and I'll follow," I suggested. And I repeated to her the old saw about how Ginger Rogers had to do everything that Fred Astaire did, only backwards in high heels. (The implication being that though ballroom dancing was ostensibly sexist, it was actually implicitly an arena of female power.)

But curiously, she didn't want to try it that way. Not, I knew, out of any allegiance to what her generation had been taught to call "gender roles" or of deference to her dad, but rather out of ironic affection for the old game, for the ritualized steps and formal diction of movement in dancing. She wanted to honor the antique steps and the ancient pattern even as they receded in meaning, honor the form even as it emptied of content. It was an exercise in retro role-playing whose charm lay in its complete irrelevance to ordinary life in the twenty-first century. Being queer and out made her *more* eager to learn the foxtrot as they used to do it, just as feeling wholly healthy makes us more ready to try unpasteurized wine and cheese. There was no point in subverting the foxtrot. It was not worthy of subversion. Taking the foxtrot seriously was the right way of subverting it.

We moved on, another week on that twilight Central Park terrace, to the waltz. The waltz turns out to be nothing but a box. A four-step movement of your feet; left, forward, right, slide; then left, forward, right, slide. You trace a box on the floor while holding hands and heads high, and suddenly it feels like the blue Danube is streaming outside your window. And then again, while Steve plays Sinatra's waltz, "Mam'selle." *Left foot forward, right foot slide; right foot forward, left foot slide.* All of that Great Waltz stuff, all of that grace, build around this simple construction of a box on the floor. The only thing the man has to do, as the leader, is push and propel the box shape in a way that is almost invisible to anyone but the woman he is dancing with. You are, once again, one minute, sometimes one second, ahead of your partner. The other task was to be mindful of the shape of the invisible imaginary room in which you are waltzing. "Avoid the wall!" Steve would say as we moved in space. Where in boxing it was the vile, opportunity-seeking opponent one had to imagine, in dancing it was the crowd of fellow dancers watching jealously from the sidelines as you wowed them with your ease, shared only with one other.

———

WHAT I CAN'T CONVEY to those who have not taken formal dance lessons is how much its repetitive simplicity feels neither repetitive nor simple, feels instead like an entry into another world of possible patterns, as though grace had descended on your shoulder just by the act of following instructions. No recipe in cooking ever made so fine a souffle; simply following the rote instructions made your heart leap.

Olivia looked so lovely, too! Her normal slightly slouched college-girl posture suddenly straight, but not ramrod straight, as in the self-conscious way we had encouraged her "Stand up straight, kiddo!" No, this was the straightness of delight, a kind of self-confident, mischievous self-presentation that I had never seen her master before—as though her spine were filled not with metal rods but with molten mercury, strong but liquid. And she no doubt was looking at the father whom she had spent a lifetime seeing bent, neck craned, over his keyboard suddenly standing up and looking like, well, if not like Fred Astaire, at least like someone who looked you in the eye. We were together. We were both amused. We were working hard.

As time went on, I felt myself oddly split and taped together between the two activities, boxing and dancing, so alike in the four-beat physical system one had to recall and internalize—internalizing it about as poorly as anyone ever has, in my case, the system almost always remaining external. I struggled to swallow them into my inner self. Over time, the overlap and the entanglement of the three, and sometimes four, repeated steps that dancing and boxing shared became inescapable. It was like something out of a silent comedy, where Chaplin or Keaton somehow has to jump from one activity to the other—dancing with the flapper and then fighting with her brother, a quick dip and then a sudden jab, back and forth, at accelerating attention, between the two. Dancing and boxing were both articulated in exactly four distinct beats. In the gym beneath the elevated train: Jab, jab, cross—*hook*! Then the hands went back to the side of your head. On the esplanade in Central Park: Step, step, slide—*stop*! Hop or shift to change directions. Then back to the four-part sequence again. In each skill, a rich and flowing activity broken down, yet again, as so often, into component parts, the pattern built back up—in this case with this participant always feeling on the edge, never quite in the flow of it, but seeing again how the flow is never really a flow but a thing built up of limitless smaller frames, until, played rapidly, it gave the illusion of continuous movement. The manufacture of this illusion, short steps into seamless sequence, is not a special feature of the movies; it is a fact of life, the truth of learning. All the steps seemed to meld together into a single, just syncopated seamless whole—outlines only very slightly blurred, the tracks almost overlapped, with a very small echo audible. Driving and dancing, the acquisition of "the hand" and the movement of the feet; the jab of boxing and the time-tilt of drawing, form a permanent human rhythm, heartbeat-bound, of small actions building bigger blocks.

If you surrender to allow the simple pattern to imprint itself on your mind, an inordinate gift will blossom. At least, that is the promise of mastery. Commit to the steps or the tilts or the finger patterns—or for that matter to being the noodle and the bee, head in motion—and you'll achieve something that, if not exactly mastery, is at least an actual accomplishment, a happy patch, a bit of software that you had never had before. Having it now, however poorly you install it, makes yours an expanded and extended mind and body, a significantly different self from the one you were assigned at birth. Repetition and perseverance and a comical degree of commitment—simply the commitment both to recognize the absurdity of your effort and the sincerity of its goal—are disproportionately rewarded in the real world of the real work.

That is, so long as the standard of reward is interior, the chosen expenditure of your own heartbeats. When, in what one might call my late period, I manage to traverse two miles of country road at night in a car, driving by myself, I have a burst of the heart equal to any Formula 1 racer winning at the Monaco Grand Prix. (In the one thing I am devoted to doing well, paradoxically—making shapely sentences that still make sense—I am perpetually discontent, since I spy the difference between near perfection and perfection.) We adjust ourselves to our own interior experience, as whales and hummingbirds do—as birds do, mother, as Shakespeare has the young prince in *Macbeth* say about the seeming self-sufficiency of animals. They manage. This paradox of accomplishment and satisfaction is in its way restorative: it means that we can do some things badly and still feel good about having done them, and some things well and still feel badly about not doing them better. Equilibrium of the mind is achieved by doing both.

———

EVENING AFTER EVENING on the esplanade above the Wollman Rink, my daughter dancing, after a morning spent in Queens, my imaginary opponent ducking as I jab . . . If one thing weaves together our search for the real work, more even than the rule of small blocks of effort assembling surprising structures of art, it is that we almost always have a spectator or audience in mind as we do it. We engage in the perpetual play with the invisible Other. There's the obstinate spectator whose mind must be taken in by the trick; the beholder of the nude sketch who will turn the smudge into a sign of life; the listener who hears the tremor in the soprano's vibrato, her back phrase of the beat as the means to absolute emotion; even the other driver, who, seeing the Hand, will register its benevolent intentions even when a malevolent one is meant—not to mention the threatening man waiting impatiently outside the loo, who must first be imagined in order to be dismissed. To that list I could add the imaginary enemy boxer, perpetually circling, perpetually threatening, right at the end of my reach but whom I will never see and never fight.

But all of those imaginary others are ways of preparing us for the one real Other. Here was a real partner, really engaged, with the fictional ones all now pushed elsewhere. Olivia and I can't resist looking at each other, in some mix of absurdity, complicity, irony, self-knowledge, and affection. What I suspect is her affection for my affectations returning my affection for her readiness to oblige them in a pinch. We are each other's Other, the actual audience.

Emmanuel Levinas, the French Jewish philosopher, once said, gnomically, that we know ourselves only by staring into the eyes of another. This was a reproach to Descartes, who said that he knew himself by his own self-reflection. As Levinas would have it, I see another, therefore I am.

I had frankly always thought this the kind of thing so obvious that only the French would find it deep. But approaching sixty-five, it now seemed to me so deep that only an American would find it obvious. The self we keep inside is the needy monkey of Buddhist disdain. It becomes something more only in the rare moments when we dance in time with another self, looking at us. Meaning *is* the face of the Other. I see myself in my daughter's eyes. The self becomes a soul only when it sees another self. Mastery, the dream of doing things well, is merely the purpose, the long-range scheme or plan, of looking at another, with something up your sleeve—even if doing nothing grander than pleasing a partner, or a table full of friends.

The real work is what we do for other people. We define madness as mastery without an object. The magicians' essential murmur is that the subject is . . . the subject! The magicians table talk all turns on the modest business of amusing an audience; we can't make art without one, and the sadness of the artist is only in not finding at least one other to amuse. (Vincent van Gogh had his brother Theo; that was enough.) There is no magic without a master. But also, no magic without a mark. We love to do things because when we do, we are no longer things. We are selves and, sometimes, souls. With time and luck perhaps to dance, the poet writes, having first had us stumble and then step. But stepping and stumbling *are* dancing, segments becoming seamless.

Time and luck? Bullshit, perhaps. Time is no one's luck; it ravages us all. Still, the city rat rustles in the bushes, the lights rise in the Central Park skyline, the teacher, who must be paid, soon presses down on my back, we lead and follow and, somehow, however badly, my daughter upright in my arms, we dance.

The Seventh Mystery
of Mastery,
Resolved

Well, we seem to dance; we have the *intention* of dancing; we *feel* inside as if we're dancing; we are *seen* to dance, I have not yet aged past the point of dancing . . .

No! We *do*, close enough to count as realized work. We dance.

ACKNOWLEDGMENTS

I HAVE FIRST OF ALL TO THANK MY TEACHERS, WHO willy-nilly, and sometimes topsy-turvy, made this book: Arturo Leon, Joey Contrada, Jacob Collins, Steve Dane, Dan Rocker, Jamy Ian Swiss—and of course my mother, Myrna Gopnik. My old friend and sparring partner, Jerry Coyne, and my new friends from North Carolina State, Lauren Nichols and Rob Dunn, were hugely generous with their time and explanatory detailing of human plumbing and hummingbird heartbeats.

Henry Finder, at *The New Yorker*, and Dan Gerstle, in these pages, both shaped, chauffeured, and silently improved and amended these stories. Both are masters of the quiet and patient art of editing, particularly of noisy and exigent authors.

Many fact-checkers from *The New Yorker* took on the slipped spellings and misdated moments original to these essays. I thank them all. Emily Yang, still with that intimidating bureau of the gently omniscient, was kind enough to take another Argus-eyed look at what hadn't been checked before. All mistakes remain my own.

Lorinda Ash, Eric Fischl, April Gornik, and Jonathan Zimmerman were hugely generous in helping a harried author find places to work in peace though, blessedly, not in quiet. I am grateful to their shared spaces, and to their stereos (as I still, antiquely, call all music machines.)

Alison, Morgan, Blake, Hilary and Melissa haunt these pages, as ever, with their own parallel and instructive efforts.

And Martha, Luke, and Olivia, as always.

CREDITS